CHURCHILL
The Life
An Authorized Pictorial Biography

Max Arthur

FIREFLY BOOKS

For Sir Martin Gilbert, my
friend and inspiration.

A FIREFLY BOOK

Published by Firefly Books Ltd. 2015

First printing

Publisher Cataloging-in-Publication Data (U.S.)

Arthur, Max, 1939-
    Churchill : the life / Max Arthur. [272] pages : color photographs ; cm.
Summary: "A biography of Churchill in honor of 50 years since his death, including
photographs and his own personal writings" – Provided by publisher.
ISBN-13: 978-1-77085-632-5
1. Churchill, Winston, 1874-1965. 2. Great Britain – Politics and government – 20th
century. 3. Prime ministers — Great Britain - Biography. I. Title.
941.084/092 dc23   DA566.9.C5A744 2015

Library and Archives Canada Cataloguing in Publication

Arthur, Max, 1939-, author
    Churchill : the life / Max Arthur.
Includes bibliographical references and index.
ISBN 978-1-77085-632-5 (bound)
    1. Churchill, Winston, 1874-1965. 2. Churchill, Winston, 1874-1965— Pictorial
works. 3. Churchill, Winston, 1874-1965—Quotations. 4. Churchill, Winston, 1874-
1965—Anecdotes. 5. Prime ministers—Great Britain--Biography. 6. Statesmen--Great
Britain--Biography. 7. Politicians—Great Britain—Biography. 8. Great Britain—
Politics and government—20th century. I. Title.
DA566.9.C5A78 2015   941.084092   C2015-903764-6

Published in the United States by
Firefly Books (U.S.) Inc.
P.O. Box 1338, Ellicott Station
Buffalo, New York 14205

Published in Canada by
Firefly Books Ltd.
50 Staples Avenue, Unit 1
Richmond Hill, Ontario L4B 0A7

Printed in China

First published in Great Britain in 2015 by Cassell, a
division of Octopus Publishing Group Ltd
Carmelite House
50 Victoria Embankment
London EC4Y 0DZ
www.octopusbooks.co.uk

Published in association with Churchill Heritage Ltd

Editorial Director Trevor Davies
Art Director Juliette Norsworthy
Designer David Rowley
Senior Editor Alex Stetter
Copy Editor Caroline Taggart
Picture Researcher Jennifer Veall
Production Controller John Casey

The right of Max Arthur to be identified as the author
of this Work has been asserted by him in accordance
with the Copyright, Designs & Patents Act 1988.

Contents

Introduction

For this book, I have sought out a number of unseen photographs of Winston Churchill and, rather than simply describe them in a one- or two-line caption, I have tried to convey the background to the event and to capture Churchill's feelings at the time the photograph was taken. I have used his own words or the words of those close to him, or against him, to enhance the images.

Churchill: The Life also contains copies of his great speeches and facsimiles of his letters – sometimes acerbic, sometimes boisterous, but always enlightening. We discover how difficult and disenchanting Churchill found life at school and how he pleaded with his mother and father to show him some affection. We see how his confidence grew at Sandhurst and his reputation develops during his adventures as a young soldier and war correspondent. We observe how, on his entry into Parliament, he began a whole new and successful life, which was eventually overshadowed by the Dardanelles Campaign. Churchill's time serving in the trenches of the Great War is vividly portrayed by those who served alongside him.

Throughout the book I have tried to capture the basis of his emotional life with his wife Clementine and their family.

Clementine certainly had the patience of a saint, but their letters, from the early days of their courtship until the end of his life, were never less than tender. Clementine was at times tough in her response to Winston's wild dreams, yet she was also comforting, particularly during his years in the political wilderness, when he saw himself as abandoned and held in ridicule for pointing out the inexorable rise of Nazi Germany.

Churchill's many trips to America before, during and after the war were in his view essential to the nation's defence. They were also a source of income and of inspiration, but it was his home life, at Chartwell, and his love of Clementine that truly sustained him.

The sense of destiny that had been with him since adolescence sustained him through the wilderness years and was vindicated in 1940, when, at the age of 65, he became Prime Minister in his country's time of greatest need. This book endeavours to capture the life of a man whose abounding confidence and belief in victory steadied the hearts of a nation, even long after the war was won.

While at Harrow, Winston, like all 16-year-old boys, discussed his hopes and expectations for the future with his friends. Murland de Grasse Evans remembered a conversation with him:

'Will you go into the army?' I asked.

'I don't know, it is probable, but I shall have great adventures beginning soon after I leave here.'

'Are you going into politics? Following your famous father?'

'I don't know, but it is more than likely because, you see, I am not afraid to speak in public.'

'You do not seem at all clear about your intentions or your desires.'

'That may be, but I have a wonderful idea of where I shall be eventually. I have dreams about it.'

'Where is that?' I enquired.

'Well, I can see vast changes coming over a now peaceful world; great upheavals, terrible struggles; wars such as one cannot imagine; and I tell you London will be in danger – London will be attacked and I shall be very prominent in the defence of London.'

'How can you talk like that?' I said; 'we are for ever safe from invasion, since the days of Napoleon.'

'I see further ahead than you do. I see into the future. This country will be subjected somehow, to a tremendous invasion, by what means I do not know, but (warming up to his subject) I tell you I shall be in command of the defences of London and I shall save London and England from disaster.'

'Will you be a general, then, in command of the troops?'

'I don't know; dreams of the future are blurred but the main objective is clear. I repeat – London will be in danger and in the high position I shall occupy, it will fall to me to save the Capital and save the Empire.'

1

Childhood:
1874–1892

'She shone for me like the Evening Star. I loved her dearly – but at a distance,' wrote Winston Churchill of his glamorous mother.

Lady Randolph Churchill

As a 19-year-old, American heiress Jennie Jerome had captivated young Lord Randolph Churchill during a ball on HMS *Ariadne*. Within three days the 24-year-old aristocrat had proposed, and the couple married on 15 April 1874.

The young diplomat Edgar Vincent, later Viscount D'Abernon, memorably recalled seeing Jennie for the first time in Dublin in the late 1870s:

'A dark, lithe figure, standing somewhat apart and appearing to be of another texture to those around her, radiant, translucent, intense. A diamond star in her hair, her favourite ornament – its lustre dimmed by the flashing glory of her eyes. More of the panther than of the woman in her look, but with a cultivated intelligence unknown to the jungle. Her courage not less great than that of her husband – fit mother for descendants of the great Duke. With all these attributes of brilliancy, such kindliness and high spirits that she was universally popular. Her desire to please, her delight in life, and the genuine wish that all should share her joyous faith in it, made her centre of a devoted circle.'

Such brilliance and kindliness, however, did not extend to spending much time with her infant sons in their nursery, and Winston saw little of his mother during his childhood. Their relationship would become much closer after Randolph's death in 1895.

Lord Randolph Churchill

Lord Randolph Henry Spencer-Churchill was the third son of the 7th Duke of Marlborough and Lady Frances Vane. In 1874, aged just 25, he was elected to Parliament as the member for Woodstock, shortly before Winston's birth. He would serve as Chancellor of the Exchequer, Leader of the House of Commons and Secretary of State for India before his death at the age of 45.

The young, affection-starved Winston deeply admired his father, but found him as emotionally distant as his mother. 'To me he seemed to own the key to everything...worth having,' he wrote in a later memoir. 'But if ever I began to show the slightest idea of comradeship, he was immediately offended.'

However, Randolph was unquestionably Winston's political inspiration. Shortly after his father's death, Winston told *Strand Magazine*, he 'read industriously every word he had ever spoken and learnt by heart large portions of his speeches... He seemed to me to have possessed in the days of his prime the key alike to popular oratory and political action... Although a loyal Tory, he was in fact during the whole of his political life...a liberal-minded man.'

Elsewhere he wrote of the catastrophe of his father's early death: 'All my dreams of comradeship with him, of entering Parliament at his side and in his support, were ended. There remained for me only to pursue his aims and vindicate his memory.'

'When does one first begin to remember?'
wrote Churchill. 'When do the waving lights
and shadows of dawning consciousness cast
their print upon the mind of a child?"

A painted cameo of Winston as a baby

Winston Churchill was born on
30 November 1874. His parents had
planned for their son to be born at
their London home on Charles Street,
but he arrived, reportedly six weeks
prematurely, while the couple were
staying at Blenheim Palace, the
Oxfordshire residence of the Dukes
of Marlborough. Randolph described
the unexpected nature of Winston's
birth in a letter to his mother-in-law:

'She [Jennie] had a fall on Tuesday
walking with the shooters, and a
rather imprudent and rough drive
in a pony carriage brought on the
pains on Saturday night. We tried
to stop them, but it was no use. They
went on all Sunday. Of course the
Oxford physician did not come. We
telegraphed for the London man,
Dr Hope, but he did not arrive till this
morning. The country Dr is however
a clever man, and the baby was safely
born at 1.30 this morning after about
8 hours of labour.'

However, another account, by
Jennie's sister, told how Jennie was
dancing at a ball held in the great
ballroom before her contractions
started. There was no time to find
a suitable bedroom and so Winston
was born in a nearby room, which
that night had been turned into a
temporary cloakroom.

Portrait of Winston aged five

Before Winston's second birthday the family moved to Ireland, where the Prime Minister, Benjamin Disraeli, had appointed his grandfather as Lord-Lieutenant. Randolph Churchill accompanied his father as secretary, and for nearly three years the family lived in a house called 'The Little Lodge'. Here, at the age of five, Winston sat for a portrait.

Ringlets of Winston's hair, preserved in the Birth Room at Blenheim Palace

'My nurse was my confidante. Mrs Everest it was who looked after me and tended all my wants. It was to her I poured out many troubles'.

Winston's nurse Mrs Everest, whom he affectionately called 'Woom' or 'Woomany'

'My nurse was my confidante. Mrs Everest it was who looked after me and tended all my wants. It was to her I poured out many troubles... Before she came to us, she had brought up for 12 years a little girl called Ella, the daughter of a clergyman who lived in Cumberland. "Little Ella", though I never saw her, became a feature of my life. I knew all about her; what she liked to eat; how she used to say her prayers; in what ways she was naughty and in what ways she was good. I had a vivid picture in my mind of her home in the North country. I was also taught to be very fond of Kent. It was, Mrs Everest said, "the garden of England". She had been born at Chatham, and was immensely proud of Kent. No county could compare with Kent, any more than any other country could compare with England. Ireland, for instance, was nothing like so good. As for France, Mrs Everest, who had at one time wheeled me in my perambulator up and down what she called the "Shams Elizzie", thought very little of it. Kent was the place. Its capital was Maidstone, and all round Maidstone there grew strawberries, cherries, raspberries and plums. Lovely! I always wanted to live in Kent.'

Winston aged two, with his mother, 1876

Winston had arrived in Dublin dressed, as was the fashion, like a girl. At that time boys and girls were dressed alike for the first few years of their lives, a custom that continued until the period of austerity following the First World War. Winston's frilly petticoats were gradually replaced by more boyish attire. Later his mother was to write to her husband, who went to London from time to time to attend Parliament:

'Winston is flourishing tho' rather X the last 2 days more teeth I think...'

'Winston has just been with me – such a darling he is – "I can't have my Mama go – & if she does I will run after the train & jump in," he said to me. I have told Everest to take him out for a drive tomorrow if it is fine – as it is better the stables shd have a little work...'

'I bought Winston an elephant this afternoon which he has been asking me for some time, & I was on the point of saying to the shop-woman "An ephelant." I just stopped myself in time...'

Winston in Dublin at the age of five, with his mother's sister Leonie (later Lady Leslie)

'It was at "The Little Lodge" I was first menaced with Education,' Winston later wrote. 'The approach of a sinister figure described as "the Governess" was announced. Her arrival was fixed for a certain day. In order to prepare for this day Mrs. Everest produced a book called *Reading without Tears*. It certainly did not justify its title in my case. I was made aware that before the Governess arrived I must be able to read without tears...

'We toiled each day. My nurse pointed with a pen at the different letters. I thought it all very tiresome. Our preparations were by no means completed when the fateful hour struck and the governess was due to arrive. I did what so many oppressed peoples have done in similar circumstances: I took to the woods. I hid in the extensive shrubberies – forests they seemed – which surrounded "The Little Lodge". Hours passed before I was retrieved and handed over to "the Governess".'

Right: **Winston in a sailor suit, 1881**
His parents left Dublin in 1880, taking
Winston and his baby brother, who
had been born in February, with them
to London to prepare for the general
election which saw his father re-
elected. At Easter 1882 Winston was at
Blenheim and from there his beloved
nurse took him to the Isle of Wight,
where her sister lived:

'When I first stayed at Ventnor
we were fighting a war with the
Zulus...They killed a great many of
our soldiers, but judging from the
pictures, not nearly so many as our
soldiers killed of them. I was very
angry with the Zulus, and glad to hear
they were being killed...After a while
it seemed that they were all killed,
because this particular war came to
an end and there were no more
pictures of the Zulus in the papers.'

On another occasion, 'we saw a great
splendid ship with all her sails set,
passing the shore only a mile or two
away. "That is a troopship," they said,
"bringing the men back from the war."
... Then all of a sudden there were black
clouds and wind and the first drop of a
storm, and we just scrambled home....
The next time I went out on those cliffs
there was no splendid ship in full sail,
but three black masts were pointed out
to me, sticking up out of the water in
a stark way. She was the *Eurydice*. She
had capsized in this very squall and
gone to the bottom with three hundred
soldiers on board. The divers went
down to bring up the corpses. I was
told – and it made a scar on my mind
– that some of the divers had fainted
with terror at seeing the fish eating
the bodies of the poor soldiers who
had been drowned just as they were
coming back home after all their hard
work and danger in fighting savages.'

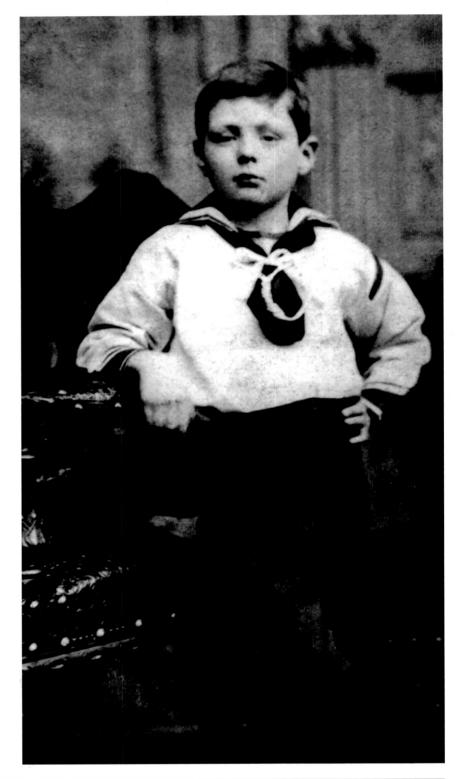

Opposite: **Winston, 1885**

'Much worse peril began to threaten. I was to go to school. I was now seven years old. And I was what grown-up people in their off-hand way called a "troublesome boy".'

Churchill.

S. GEORGE'S SCHOOL,
ASCOT.

Report from March 1st to April 9th 1884

(school report form, handwritten entries)

Report from 1 March to 9 April 1884, St George's School, Ascot

Composition: Improved
Translation: Improved
Grammar: Improved
Diligence: Conduct has been exceedingly bad. He's not to be trusted to do any one thing. He has however notwithstanding made decided progress.
No. of times late: 20. Very disgraceful
History and Geography: Very good, especially History
General conduct: Very bad – is a constant trouble to everybody and is always in some scrape or other.

'How I hated this school, and what a life of anxiety I lived,' Winston was to write later about St George's. 'I made very little progress at my lessons, and none at all at games. I counted the days and the hours to the end of every term, when I should return home from this hateful servitude and range my soldiers in line of battle on the nursery floor.

'The greatest pleasure I had in those days was reading. When I was nine and a half my father gave me *Treasure Island*, and I remember the delight with which I devoured it. My teachers saw me at once backward and precocious, reading books beyond my years and yet at the bottom of the Form. They were offended. They had large resources of compulsion at their disposal, but I was stubborn. Where my reason, imagination or interests were not engaged, I would not or I could not learn.'

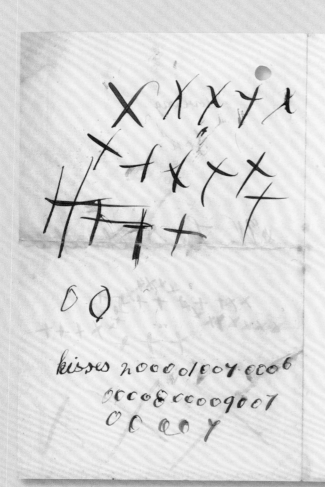

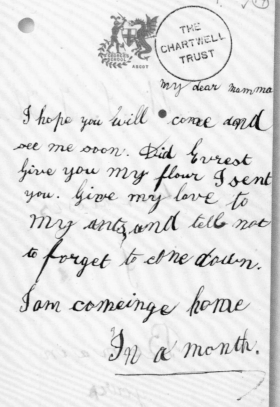

my dear mamma

I hope you will come and see me soon. Did Evrest give you my flour I sent you. Give my love to my ants and tell not to forget to come down.

I am comeinge home In a month.

kisses

A letter from Winston to his mother, 1883
It looks as if young Winston was writing this letter unsupervised and from the heart. Other letters from the school are written much more neatly. Here he begs his mother to visit him and covers the page with hugs and kisses (crosses and circles).

'This was a smaller school than the one I had left. It was also cheaper and less pretentious. But there was an element of kindness and of sympathy which I had found conspicuously lacking in my first experience.'

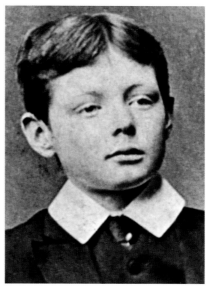

Left: **Pupils and staff at Churchill's boarding school in Brighton, run by the Misses Thomson**
As a young boy Churchill suffered from repeated bouts of ill health, so much so that the family doctor advised that he should leave St George's in Ascot (which Churchill called St James's in his memoirs) and go to a school by the sea.

Above: **Winston Churchill, 1884**
Churchill later wrote in *My Early Life*:
' Our family doctor, the celebrated Robson Roose, then practised at Brighton; and as I was now supposed to be very delicate, it was thought desirable that I should be under his constant care. I was accordingly, in 1883, transferred to a school at Brighton kept by two ladies.
'This was a smaller school that the one I had left. It was also cheaper and less pretentious. But there was an element of kindness and of sympathy which I had found conspicuously lacking in my first experience. Here I remained for three years; and though I very nearly died from an attack of double pneumonia, I got gradually much stronger in that bracing air and gentle surroundings. At this school I was allowed to learn things which interested me: French, History, lots of Poetry by heart, and above all Riding and Swimming. The impression of those years makes a pleasant picture in my mind, in strong contrast to my earlier schooldays memories.'

'Darling Mummy I despair,' Churchill wrote in a letter home while he was at Harrow. 'I'm so wretched. I don't know what to do. Don't be angry I am so miserable.'

1888 April			
Spicer Edward Samuel	Oct 19.73	E.S. Esq. 188 Cromwell Road, SW
Hay Charles Thomas	May 27.74	C.A.H. Esq. 127 Harley Street, W
Brewis Robert Henry Watkin	Sept. 29.73	P.R.B. Esq. Ibstone, Tetsworth, Oxon
Brown-Morison Basil	Dec 7.75	J.B-M. Esq. The Old House, Harrow
Campbell-Colquhoun Archibald John	March 7.74	Rev J.E.C.C. Chartwell, Westerham, Kent
Hunt Edmund Henderson	Nov 23.74	J.M.H. Esq. 4 Airlie Gardens, Campden Hill
Bodley George Hamilton	Sept 14.73	G.J.B. Esq. 26 Park Crescent, W
Spencer Churchill Winston Leonard	Nov 30.74	The Right Hon Lord Randolph S.C.M. 2 Connaught Place W
Williams Harry Currer	Apr. 13.74	G.E.W. Esq. Braeside Altrincham Cheshire
Field Edward Wheeler	May 9.73	R.E.W.F. Esq. Aspley Hall nr Nottingham
E.S. Schwann Frederick	Feb 14.74	J.F.S. Esq. Oakfield, Wimbledon
Oliver George Sydney	July 16.74	Major Gen-l Ballycroy Ballina

Harrow School register of pupils and their next of kin
Churchill entered Harrow School as a boarder in April 1888. This extract from the Admissions Register is part of the 1822–1892 volume. Every boy who was admitted to Harrow was recorded in a handwritten register like this. Entries tended to include the boy's name, date of birth, current address and father's name. Sometimes they also noted the boarding houses which boys entered and the name of the master in charge.

Lady Randolph Churchill with her sons, Winston and Jack, in London, 1889
By this time, Winston was at Harrow.

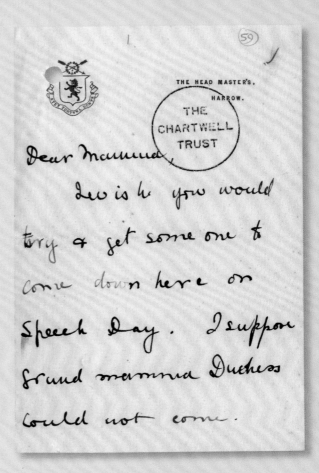

Letter from Winston to his mother, December 1891

My darling Mummy,
Welldon [the headmaster] whom I have just seen says 'I am going to let you go home for the Sunday and that's all.' He says one thing to you, but quite another to me. If he doesn't let me come home till Sat. I do hope you will let me have 2 or 3 more days. Darling Mummy, do attend to my letter. I am so wretched. Even now I weep. Please my darling Mummy be kind to your loving son. Don't let my silly letters make you angry. Let me at least think that you love me. – Darling Mummy I despair. I'm so wretched. I don't know what to do. Don't be angry I am so miserable.

Please don't expect me to go on Monday if he doesn't let me come till then. Oh how I wish I had not believed him. How I have been tricked. I don't know what to do. Do please write something kind to me. I am very sorry if I have 'riled' you before. I did only want to explain things from my point of view.
Good Bye my darling Mummy.
With best love I remain, Ever your loving son
WINSTON.

Letter from Winston to his mother, June 1891

Dear Mamma,
I wish you would try & get someone to come down here on Speech Day. I suppose grand mamma Duchess could not come.
Try and get Auntie Clara to come if no inconvenience to her. Do get someone as I shall be awfully 'out of it' if no one comes. Next Thursday is Speech Day.
Please try and arrange something darling Mummy. I hope to be able to spend Lord's at Banstead with you. Jack will probably be well enough by then.
Good bye Mamma with Love & Kisses
I remain Your loving son
WINSTON S. CHURCHILL

'This interlude at school', Churchill wrote of his time at Harrow, 'makes a sombre grey patch upon the chart of my journey. It was an unending spell of worries that did not seem petty.'

Roll call or 'bill' at Harrow, with Winston third from the left
'The Harrow custom of calling the roll is different from that of Eton. At Eton the boys stand in a cluster and lift their hats when their names are called. At Harrow they file past a Master in the school yard and answer one by one. My position was therefore revealed in its somewhat invidious humility... I frequently heard the irrelevant comment, "Why, he's last of all!"'

The old fourth form room at Harrow
'[Harrow] was an unending spell of worries that did not seem petty,' Churchill wrote, 'and of toil uncheered by fruition; a time of discomfort, restriction and purposeless monotony.'

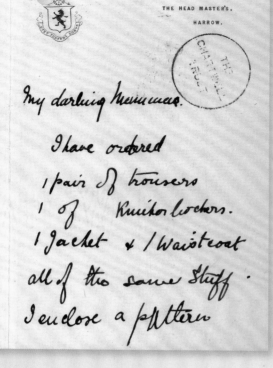

My darling Mamma.

I have ordered
1 pair of trousers
1 of Knickerbockers.
1 Jacket & 1 Waistcoat
all of the same Stuff.
I enclose a pattern

it is one which will look very well when made into [drawing] & also do to wear on Sunday [drawing] with Etons – it also looks well when [drawing] the Jacket Waistcoat & Trousers are worn.

They have not yet begun to make it so you can change it if you wish. They fully understand the making of Knee Breeches.

nice & Bagsy over knee

A letter from Winston to his mother, c.1890
Winston would often include drawings within his letters.
Here he is asking his mother's advice about the trousers,
knickerbockers, 'nice and bagsy over knee', jacket and
waistcoat that he wanted to buy. He also enclosed a sample
of the cloth that he wanted.

'I thought my father with his experience and flair had discerned in me the qualities of military genius. But I was told later that he had only come to the conclusion that I was not clever enough to go to the Bar.'

Below and opposite: **Harrow School Rifle Corps**

The Corps' tactics in mock battles were not impressive, as J.W.S. Tomlin, the head of the school, was later to recall:

'Sergeant Grisdale, a fine specimen of the old army, used to drill a small squad every morning in the school yard, but very few kept their drills, and the field days, though jolly picnics, were often ludicrous from a military point of view. I remember on one occasion during a sham flight in Cassiobury Park, Watford, a master who was captain of the corps, tying a white handkerchief to the point of his sword, and going out of his company shouting to the enemy who were in close formation about fifty yards off: "Gentlemen, I maintain that you are all dead men."'

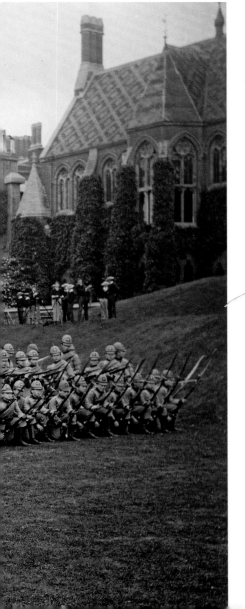

Above: **Head Master's House, Harrow School, 1892**

Winston Churchill is seen here at the age of 17, peering at the photographer over the railings of the staircase to the left of his classmate George Philip Gurney Hoare. Many of the young men who gathered for this annual school photograph went on to distinguish themselves in the First World War. Hoare was badly wounded and died in hospital aged 39. Of the 2,917 Harrovians who served in the war, 642 lost their lives.

Churchill would later write about his own military career, remembering a conversation he had with his father at the age of 14:

'This orientation was entirely due to my collection of soldiers. I had ultimately nearly fifteen hundred.

'The day came when my father himself paid a formal visit of inspection. All the troops were arranged in the correct formation of attack. He spent twenty minutes studying the scene – which was really impressive – with a keen eye and captivating smile. At the end he asked me if I would like to go into the Army. I thought it would be splendid to command an Army, so I said "Yes" at once: and immediately I was taken at my word. For years I thought my father with his experience and flair had discerned in me the qualities of military genius. But I was told later that he had only come to the conclusion that I was not clever enough to go to the Bar. However that may be, the toy soldiers turned the current of my life.'

'If you would only trace out a plan of action for yourself & carry it out & be determined to do so – I am sure you could accomplish anything you wished,' wrote Churchill's mother to her 15-year-old son.

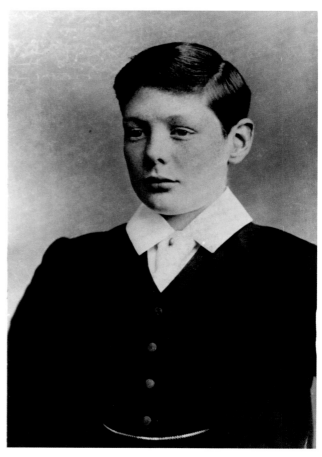

Winston as a schoolboy, c.1889
Churchill's school reports caused his parents continual anxiety. On 12 June 1890 his mother wrote to him: '...your work is an insult to your intelligence. If you would only trace out a plan of action for yourself & carry it out & be determined to do so – I am sure you could accomplish anything you wished. It is that thoughtlessness of yours which is your greatest enemy.'

Winston dressed as a junior boy at Harrow
A fellow student at Harrow School at the time Winston was a pupil wrote to *The Times* in 1928:
'If your mother wrote to ask if she could come down to see you, you told her what hat to wear, and if her figure was beyond the accepted standard, you suggested postponement; and above all, there should be no form of endearment. Mr. Winston Churchill invited his old nurse down for a day at Harrow to her intense happiness; she arrived in an old poke bonnet, her figure had attained ample proportions, and Mr. Churchill walked arm-in-arm with her in the street! It is about the nicest thing a Harrow boy has ever done.'

The Harrow punishment book

This extract from the Harrow punishment book is taken from a larger volume (1889–1965). Entries less than a hundred years old are closed to the public due to their personal nature. Punishment books were used to record the 'crimes' that boys committed (more often than not, the rules which they disobeyed) and the punishments that were meted out to offenders. Entries also include the name of the offending boy and of the master who delivered the punishment. Note that both misdemeanours and punishments are quite wide ranging: offences included lateness, rudeness and lighting a match in school. Churchill is listed here for 'breaking into premises & doing damage', the punishment for which was flogging.

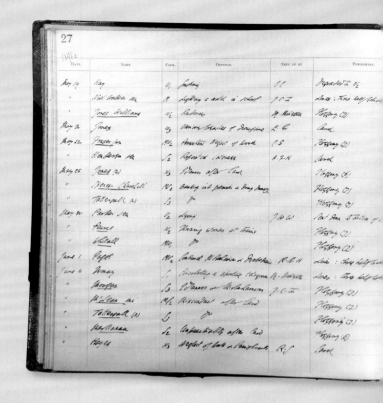

Sketch for a battle plan

These battle plans for an imaginary invasion of Russia by British forces were part of a school essay Churchill wrote in 1889. This 16-page manuscript was kept by Robert Somervell, a Harrow master who was an astute and thoughtful mentor in English and History to Winston.

Later in life Winston developed a love for painting, which possibly could have started here with these sketches.

Dear Lady Randolph Churchill.

After a good deal of hesitation and discussion with his form-master, I have decided to allow Winston to have his Treat: but I must own that he has not deserved it. I do not think, nor does Mr Somervell, that he is in any way wilfully troublesome: but his forgetfulness, carelessness, unpunctuality, and irregularity in every way, have really been so serious, that I write to ask you, when he is at home to speak very gravely to him on the subject.

When a boy first comes to [...] ability goes he ought to be at the top of his form. Whereas he is at the bottom. Yet I do not think he is idle: only his energy is fitful, and when he sets to his work it is generally too late for him to do it well. I thought it wd do him good to spend a day with you, and have therefore let him go: but unless he mends his ways, he will really have to be heavily punished. and I cannot help thinking he does not deserve any special treat during the [...] I have written very plainly to you, as I do think it very serious that he should have acquired such phenomenal slovenliness. At his age, very great improvement is possible if he seriously gives his mind to conquering his tendencies:

Letter from H.O.D. Davidson, Winston's house master for his first three terms at Harrow, to Lady Randolph Churchill, 12 July 1888

Winston, I am sorry to say, has, if anything got worse as the term passed. Constantly late for school. Losing his books, and papers, and various other things in which I need not enter – he is so regular in his irregularity, that I really don't know what to do: and sometimes think he cannot help it. But if he is unable to conquer this slovenliness (for I think all the complaints I have to make of him can be grouped under this head, though it takes various forms), he will never make a success of a public school. I hope you will take the opportunity to impress upon him very strongly the necessity of putting a check on himself in these matters, and trying to be more businesslike.

As far as ability goes he ought to be at the top of his form, whereas he is at the bottom. Yet I do not think he is idle: only his energy is fitful, and when he gets to his work it is generally too late for him to do it well. I thought it wd do him good to spend a day with you, and have therefore let him go: but unless he mends his ways, he will really have to be heavily punished... He is remarkable in many ways, and it would be a thousand pities if such good abilities were made useless by habitual negligence.

While at Harrow, Winston twice failed his exams for entry into Sandhurst and it was decided that he should go to a 'crammer' run by a Captain James. However, before he could start there he had to recover from a near fatal accident he had suffered while at his aunt's estate at Bournemouth.

Winston and his brother Jack, on holiday, 1892
In the winter of 1892, Winston visited his aunt, Lady Wimborne, at Bournemouth. Churchill later wrote, '[T]hrough the middle [of the estate] there fell to the sea level a deep cleft called a "chine". Across this "chine" a rustic bridge nearly 50 yards long had been thrown. I was just 18 and on my holidays. My younger brother aged 12, and a cousin aged 14, proposed to chase me. After I had been hunted for twenty minutes ...I decided to cross the bridge. Arrived at its centre I saw to my consternation that my pursuers had divided their forces. One stood at each end of the bridge; capture seemed certain. But in a flash there came across me a great project. The chine which the bridge spanned was full of young fir trees. Their slender tops reached to the level of the footway. "Would it not," I asked myself, "be possible to leap on to one of them and slip down the pole-like stem, breaking off each tier of branches as one descended, until the fall was broken?" I looked at it. I computed it. I meditated.... To plunge or not to plunge, that was the question! In a second I had plunged, throwing out my arms to embrace the summit of the fir tree. The argument was correct; the data were absolutely wrong. It was three days before I regained consciousness and more than three months before I crawled from my bed.'

However hard on him his parents may have been while Winston had been at school, they now responded to his accident with urgency and compassion and thought nothing of the financial outlay. Churchill later wrote, 'My father travelled over at full express from Dublin. He brought with him the greatest of London surgeons.'

2

A Young Soldier:
1893–1900

Churchill with his fellow cadets at Royal Military College, Sandhurst, 1894

On 3 September 1893, after three days as a cadet at Sandhurst, Winston wrote to his father: 'The Discipline is extremely strict – Far stricter than Harrow. Hardly any law is given to juniors on joining. No excuse is ever taken – not even with a plea of "didn't know" after the first few hours: and of course no such thing as unpunctuality or untidiness is tolerated. Still there is something very exhilarating in the military manner in which everything works; and I think that I shall like my life here during the next 18 months very much.'

He was to write later: 'At Sandhurst I had a new start. I was no longer handicapped by past neglect of Latin, French or Mathematics. We had now to learn fresh things and we all started equal. Tactics, Fortification, Topography (mapmaking), Military Law and Military Administration formed the whole curriculum. In addition were Drill, Gymnastics and Riding. No one need play any game unless he wanted to. Discipline was strict and the hours of study and parade were long. One was very tired at the end of the day. I was deeply interested in my work, especially Tactics and Fortification.'

Having left Harrow and recovered from his near-death experience, Winston just managed to pass the entry examination for Sandhurst in 1893 and was overjoyed to do so.

Churchill dressed as a pierrot at Sandhurst after the Half-Mile Donkey Race, 11 May 1894

Two days before this picture was taken, Winston had written to his mother: 'Please try to get me a costume and send it by the guard of the train at 11.45. I will meet it. Try to get a gorilla or something amusing.'

His mother sent him a more appropriate costume. The pierrots, buffoon figures who wore long-sleeved white robes, were part of every late-Victorian seaside resort entertainment. They were much enjoyed for their subversive and astute observations on society and on human foibles, as well as on themes such as love and jealousy. Winston's insightful mother had chosen well and anticipated her son's early romantic adventures. The most famous of the pierrots was Pedrolino, who was usually hopelessly in love with a beautiful but fickle woman.

Letter from Randolph Churchil, 21 April 1894

In the grounds of Sandhurst in April 1894, while Winston was picking up a stick, a fob watch his father had given to him fell into a stream. He immediately took off his clothes and dived in to try to find it, but without success. The next day he paid to have the stream dredged, but again to no avail.

Determined to find the watch, he hired 23 soldiers from the Sandhurst infantry detachment to dig a fresh channel for the stream. He then borrowed a fire engine from the local station to pump out the stream pool and the watch (pictured opposite) was eventually recovered. In great relief, Winston sent it to the London watchmaker E M Dent for repairs.

To Winston's surprise his father wrote to him a few days later:

I heard something about you yesterday which annoyed me & vexed me very much. I was at Mr Dent's about my watch, and he told me of the shameful way in which you had misused the very valuable watch I gave you. He told me you had sent it to him some time ago, having with the utmost carelessness dropped it on a stone pavement and broken it badly. The repairs of it cost £3:15s which you will have to pay Mr Dent. He then told me he had received the watch the other day and that you told him it had been dropped in the water... I would not believe you could be such a young stupid. It was clear you are not to be trusted with a valuable watch...you had better buy one of those cheap watches for £2... Jack has had the watch I gave him longer than you have had yours; the only expense I have paid on his watch was 10s for cleaning...in all qualities of steadiness taking care of his things and never doing stupid things Jack is vastly superior.

Your vy much worried parent
Randolph S. Churchill

The curious episode of the lost fob watch in Churchill's second term at Sandhurst tells a good deal about him and his relationship with his parents.

Winston's fob watch
Winston's mother was a little more understanding of her son's predicament than his father:

Dearest Winston,
I am sorry you have got into trouble over yr watch – Papa wrote to me all about it. I must own you are awfully careless & of course Papa is angry over giving you such a valuable thing. However he wrote very kindly about you so you must not be too unhappy. Meanwhile I'm afraid you would have to go without a watch. Oh! Winny what a harum scarum fellow you are! You really must give up being so childish. I'm sending you £2 with my love. I shall scold you well when we meet.
Yr loving
Mother

After graduating from Sandhurst,
20th out of 130, in December 1894,
Churchill joined the army.

**Winston Churchill in the uniform
of a Second Lieutenant of the
4th Hussars, 1895**

After leaving Sandhurst, Churchill
was commissioned on 20 February
1895 as a Cornet (Second Lieutenant)
in the 4th Queen's Own Hussars, a
light cavalry regiment, stationed very
close to Sandhurst, at Aldershot in
Hampshire. This was in defiance of
his father's wishes: Lord Randolph
would have preferred his son to join
the infantry, because members of the
cavalry had to supply their own horses
and uniforms for the grooms, an
expense that he could not afford.

In July of that year Winston heard
that his beloved former nurse 'Woom'
was critically ill. He immediately set
off for Crouch End in north London
and on his arrival called in two doctors
and a nurse to look after her, then
travelled back to his regiment on the
midnight train. He returned directly
after the morning parade to see her
slipping away. Of her death he wrote:
'She still knew me, but she gradually
became unconscious... She had no
fears at all, and did not seem to mind
very much. She had been my dearest
and most intimate friend during the
whole of 20 years I have lived.'

Winston as a young officer in his regimental uniform, 1895

Winston took his duties very seriously, but found garrison life rather boring. Always in search of adventure and self-advancement, in December 1895, while on a protracted leave from the 4th Hussars, he sailed to Cuba, where Spanish troops were fighting the local rebels. He was happy to live and fight alongside the Spanish. This was his first taste of action and to his great pleasure he was awarded his first medal. Writing in the *Saturday Review* he noted that the Cuban rebels 'neither fight bravely nor do they use their weapons effectively'. Although he thought that the Spanish were bad, 'a Cuban government would be worse, equally corrupt, more capricious and far less stable'. British Army regulation forbade Winston from wearing his Spanish decoration for bravery on his uniform, but he did so anyway.

He was later to write of youth: 'Twenty to twenty-five! These are the years! Don't be content with things as they are. Don't take No for an answer. Never submit to failure. Do not be fobbed off with mere personal success or acceptance. You will make all kinds of mistakes; but as long as you are generous and true, and also fierce, you cannot hurt the world or even seriously distress her. She was made to be wooed and won by youth. She has lived and thrived only by repeated subjugation.'

Churchill's father died at the age of 45, when Winston was 20 years old. Winston wrote: 'At his mother's house, he lingered pitifully; until very early in the morning of the 24th of January 1895 the numbing fingers of paralysis laid that weary brain to rest.'

From left to right: Leonie Leslie, Harold Warrender, Jack Churchill, Lady Randolph and Winston Churchill, 1895
Winston was not happy at the prospect of spending years in India, for which his regiment was preparing: 'I look upon going to India as useless and unprofitable exile...utterly unattractive. Feel that I am guilty of an indolent folly that I shall regret all my life.' To his mother he wrote: 'It is useless to preach the gospel of patience to me. Others as young are making the running now and what chance have I of ever catching up?'

He sailed for India on the *Britannia* on 11 September 1896.

Winston, his brother Jack and their mother, Lady Randolph, c.1896

In 1899, four years after his father's death, Winston wrote in his book *The River War*, ostensibly about the Sudanese religious leader known as the Mahdi: 'Solitary trees, if they grow at all, grow strong; and a boy deprived of a father's care often develops, if he escapes the perils of youth, an independence and vigour of thought which may restore in after life the heavy loss of early days.' Sir Martin Gilbert, Churchill's official biographer, had little doubt that Winston was referring to his father.

In October 1896 , Winston's regiment reached Bangalore, then a small, sleepy cantonment town. He liked the climate in India: '[T]he sun even at midday is temperate and the mornings and evenings are fresh and cool.'

Churchill in Bangalore, 1896

Churchill was pleased with the house allotted to him on his arrival in Bangalore: 'a magnificent pink and white stucco palace in the middle of a large and beautiful garden'. And he was well served by his staff, who included a gardener, a water-carrier, a dhobi and a watchman.

Churchill remained in India for nearly two years, during which time he was in action on the North-West Frontier. On 19 September 1897 he wrote to his mother: 'I rode on my grey pony all along the skirmish line where everyone else was lying down in cover. Foolish perhaps but I play for high stakes and given an audience there is no act too daring or too noble. Without the gallery things are different... I should like to come back and wear my medals at some big dinner or some other function.'

He also thought a campaign in Egypt would enhance his political prospects. He pleaded with his mother to arrange for him to accompany Kitchener's advance up the Nile: 'I should not have forgiven myself if an expedition started next year and I felt it was my own fault I was not there. I revolve Egypt continuously in my mind. Two years in Egypt my dearest Mamma – with a campaign thrown in – would I think qualify me to be allowed to beat my sword into a paper cutter and my sabretache into an election address.'

TELEGRAPH, SATURDAY, OCTOBER 9, 1897.

THE WAR IN THE INDIAN HIGHLANDS.

By A YOUNG OFFICER.

NAWAGAI, Sept. 12.

In my last letter to you I gave some account of the march of a column of troops in service in India. Since then we have been continuously moving . . .

The men are so cheery and good-humoured, so anxious to get on, so eager to find the enemy, so pleased at being on active service, that it is only right that their endurance of severe hardships should be recorded. On the march the British and native regiments mutually inspire each other to exertions. The soldiers of India naturally feel the effects of the climate less than those from cooler lands. This, of course, the British infantryman will not admit . . .

When we arrived at the camping-ground this morning the camel transport was far behind, and it was necessary to wait on the bare and dusty plateau for a couple of hours, in the blaze of the sun, until the baggage should arrive. I talked to some of the Queen's Regiment—which is the English Regiment with the 3rd Brigade. The men had just marched fourteen miles with arms and ammunition, and not one had fallen out by the way. They looked strained and weary, but nothing would induce them to admit it. "An easy march," they said. "Should have been here long ago if the native troops had not kept halting." This is the material for empire-building . . .

A cutting from the *Telegraph* showing one of Churchill's articles while he was serving as a young officer in India, 9 October 1897
Churchill wrote 15 articles for the *Telegraph*, which formed the basis for his first book, *The Story of the Malakand Field Force*. He was paid five pounds per column, but was not at all pleased that the articles didn't carry his name.

Meerut, India, 1899
While in India, Churchill took up polo, a game he went on to play for the next 30 years. This photograph includes the four members of the 4th Hussars' polo team, who won the inter-regimental final in February 1899 in Meerut: Winston is standing in the back row, second from the right.

The Charge of the 21st Lancers at Omdurman
(detail), Matthew Hale (1852–1924), 1899
In July 1898 the War Office attached Lieutenant
Churchill to the 21st Lancers. The charge of the
Lancers at Omdurman in Sudan on 2 September
1898 was a battle in which he excelled himself.
This was the climax of Kitchener's expedition to
re-conquer the Sudan and avenge the murder of
General Charles Gordon nearly 14 years before.
Due to an early injury to his right shoulder
Churchill was unable to charge with a drawn
sword. Instead he used a Mauser pistol on the
Mahdist forces. After the battle he wrote to
his mother: 'I was under fire all day and rode
through the charge. You know my luck in
these things. I was about the only officer whose
clothes, saddlery, or horse were uninjured. I fired
10 shots with my pistol – all necessary – and just
got to the end of it as we cleared the crush. I never
felt the slightest nervousness and felt as cool as I
do now. I pulled up and reloaded within 30 yards
of their mass and then trotted after my troop who
were then about 100 yards away. I am sorry to
say I shot 5 men for certain and two doubtful...
Nothing touched me. I destroyed those who
molested me and so passed out without any
disturbance of body or mind.'

He was to write later: 'Nothing like the Battle
of Omdurman will ever be seen again. It was the
last link in the long chain of those spectacular
conflicts whose vivid and majestic splendour
has done so much to invest war with glamour.'

Opposite: **Churchill, c.1899**
Absolutely determined to enter politics, Churchill resigned his commission on 3 May 1899 after only four years in the army. On 20 June he was adopted as Conservative candidate for Oldham, a predominantly working-class community. In his election address four days later, he declared, 'I regard the improvement of the condition of the British people as the main end of modern government.'

Below: **Churchill is held as a prisoner of war, Pretoria, 18 November 1899**
Churchill was defeated at Oldham, but four months later war broke out between the British and the Boers. The *Morning Post* arranged for him to go to South Africa as a correspondent. At £250 a month he was believed, at the time, to be the highest paid journalist ever to go to a warfront. On 31 October 1899 he reached Cape Town. On 15 November he and his friend Captain Aylmer Haldane travelled by an armoured train for a reconnaissance of Boer-held territory. Their train was ambushed by the Boers, and derailed. Churchill set about the task of salvaging the engine. Haldane later recalled: 'For an hour efforts to clear the line were unsuccessful, as the trucks were heavy and jammed together, and the break-down gang could not be found, but Mr Churchill with indomitable perseverance continued his difficult task... I would point out that while engaged on the work of saving the engine, for which he was mainly responsible, he was frequently exposed to the full fire of the enemy. I cannot speak too highly of his gallant conduct.' They eventually got the engine moving, but Churchill, Haldane and 50 others were captured by the Boers.

After being captured by the Boers on 15 November 1899, Churchill was held in a prisoner-of-war camp – a converted school in Pretoria – from which he soon escaped.

Official instructions re arrest of Winston Spencer Churchill.

(Translation)

Office of Commissioner of Police,
PRETORIA, 20/12/99.

Honourable Sir,

Herewith I send you 3 portraits of the prisoner of war, Winston Spencer Churchill, correspondent of the "Morning Post" of London, who ran away from the State Model School here presumably between the hours of 10 o'clock on the evening of the 12th and 4 o'clock on the morning of the 13th inst. Further described as follows:-

Englishman, 25 years of age, about 5 feet 8 inches in height, medium build, stooping gait, fair complexion, reddish brown hair, almost invisible slight moustache, speaks through his nose, cannot give full expression to the letter "s", and does not know a word of Dutch. Wore a suit of brown clothes, but not uniform - an ordinary suit of clothes.

It is necessary to mention that the accompanying photograph is a copy of one taken most probably about 18 months ago. Be good enough to show the public (as far as possible) this photograph, and request your police and the burghers to keep a sharp look out for the fugitive, and if he is identified to place him under arrest at once. Should anything important come to light with regard to the said prisoner I request that you will inform me of the same without delay.

I have the honour to be,
Your obedient Servant,

The Honourable
Resident Justice of Peace,
SCHWEIZER-RENECKE.

Acty Com. of Police

Arrest warrant for Winston Churchill, 1899
The official instructions for the 'arrest of Winston Spencer Churchill' after his escape from the PoW camp, issued in Pretoria on 20 December 1899 (above right), were accompanied by a photograph of Chuchill taken during his time with the 21st Lancers (above left). In the document, the fugitive is described as an 'Englishman, 25 years of age, about 5 feet 8 inches in height, medium build, stooping gait, fair complexion, reddish brown hair, almost invisible slight moustache, speaks through his nose, cannot give full expression to the letter "s", and does not know a word of Dutch.'

A Boer official in Pretoria offered a reward of £25 'to anyone who brings the escaped prisoner of war Churchill dead or alive to this office'.

£25.—.—

(vijf en twintig pond stg.) belooning uitgeloofd door de Sub-Commissie van Wijk V voor den Specialen Constabel dezer wijk, die den ontvluchte Krijgsgevangene Churchill levend of dood te dezen kantore aflevert.—

Namens de Sub-Comm.
Wijk V
Das de Haas
Sec.

Translation.

£25

(Twenty-five Pounds stg.) REWARD is offered by the Sub-Commission of the fifth division, on behalf of the Special Constable of the said division, to anyone who brings the escaped prisoner of war

CHURCHILL,

dead or alive to this office.

For the Sub-Commission of the fifth division,
(Signed) LODK. de HAAS, Sec.

Leaflet offering a £25 reward for the capture of Winston Churchill, November 1899
As a civilian war correspondent, Churchill was not himself a significant figure to the Boers. However they would have known that his father had been an eminent politician and that his bloodline went back to beyond the Duke of Marlborough. He was therefore a valuable bargaining tool, from which the Boers hoped to get some capital.

Churchill became friendly with the man who had offered the £25 reward for his capture and, when they met later on, remarked that he could at least have made it £50.

Churchill in Durban, 23 December 1899

Churchill reached Durban on 23 December 1899, where he described his escape to an enthusiastic crowd. On the following day he set out for General Sir Redvers Buller's headquarters, having decided to join a local regiment, the South African Light Horse. On 26 December, Buller wrote to Lady Londonderry: 'Winston Churchill turned up here yesterday, escaped from Pretoria. He really is a fine fellow and I must say I admire him greatly. I wish he was leading irregular troops instead of writing for a rotten paper. We are very short of good men, as he appears to be, out here...'

Little more than a month after being taken prisoner by the Boers, Churchill was free again, as he was quick to report to *Pearson's Illustrated War News*.

HOW I ESCAPED
FROM PRETORIA.

By Winston Churchill.

THE *Morning Post* has received the following telegram from Mr. Winston Spencer Churchill, its war correspondent, who was taken prisoner by the Boers and escaped from Pretoria:

LOURENCO MARQUES, December 21st, 10 p.m.

I was concealed in a railway truck under great sacks.

I had a small store of good water with me.

I remained hidden, chancing discovery.

The Boers searched the train at Komati Poort, but did not search deep enough, so after sixty hours of misery I came safely here.

I am very weak, but I am free.

I have lost many pounds weight, but I am lighter in heart.

I shall also avail myself of every opportunity from this moment to urge with earnestness an unflinching and uncompromising prosecution of the war.

On the afternoon of the 12th the Pearson's Illustrated War News Transvaal Government's Secretary for War informed me that there was little chance of my release.

I therefore resolved to escape the same night, and left the State Schools Prison at Pretoria by climbing the wall when the sentries' backs were turned momentarily.

I walked through the streets of the town without any disguise, meeting many burghers, but I was not challenged in the crowd.

I got through the pickets of the Town Guard, and struck the Delagoa Bay Railroad.

I walked along it, evading the watchers at the bridges and culverts.

I waited for a train beyond the first station.

The out 11.10 goods train from Pretoria arrived, and before it had reached full speed I boarded with great difficulty, and hid myself under coal sacks.

I jumped from the train before dawn, and sheltered during the day in a small wood, in company with a huge vulture, who displayed a lively interest in me.

I walked on at dusk.

There were no more trains that night.

The danger of meeting the guards of the railway line continued; but I was obliged to follow it, as I had no compass or map.

I had to make wide *détours* to avoid the bridges, stations, and huts.

My progress was very slow, and chocolate is not a satisfying food.

The outlook was gloomy, but I persevered, with God's help, for five days.

The food I had to have was very precarious.

I was lying up at daylight, and walking on at night time, and, meanwhile, my escape had been discovered and my description telegraphed everywhere.

All the trains were searched.

Everyone was on the watch for me.

Four wrong people were arrested.

But on the sixth day I managed to board a train beyond Middleburg, whence there is a direct service to Delagoa.

Above: An article by Winston Churchill for *Pearson's Illustrated War News*, 1899

Opposite: Churchill in the uniform of the South African Light Horse, c.1899 Churchill wrote for the *Morning Post* of his experiences witnessing a number of battles. His words on the battle of Spion Kop were published on 17 February 1900: 'Corpses lay here and there. Many of the wounds were of a horrible nature. The splinters and fragments of the shell had torn and mutilated in the most ghastly manner. I passed about two hundred while I was climbing up. There was, moreover, a small but steady leakage of unwounded men of all corps. Some of these cursed and swore. Others were utterly exhausted and fell on the hillside in stupor. Others again seemed drunk, though they had had no liquor. Scores were sleeping heavily. Fighting was still proceeding, and stray bullets struck all over the ground, while the Maxim shell guns scourged the flanks of the hill and the sheltering Infantry at regular intervals of a minute.'

Opposite: Churchill in South Africa, working as a war correspondent for the *Morning Post*

General Buller allowed Churchill to remain a war correspondent as well as a soldier with the South African Light Horse. Not only did he fight in the battles of 1900, he also reported on them for the *Morning Post*. He is seen here at the scene of his capture in January 1900.

Above: Churchill and other war correspondents, aboard the RMS *Dunottar Castle* in July 1900

Seen here seated second from left, Churchill was travelling home to England on the same ship that had brought him to South Africa eight months earlier. Immediately above him is his friend J. B. Atkins, of the *Manchester Guardian*, who later published *The Relief of Ladysmith*, based on his experiences of the Boer War.

Winston Churchill was elected as the Member of Parliament for Oldham on 1 October 1900, two months before his 26th birthday.

A prophecy fulfilled

Harpers, 1900

"Somewhat heavy-looking, ambitious, hard-working, with a touch of mysticism that attracts the mob, a born orator, with power to move people as he wills, Winston Spencer Churchill must go far. To-day he is only twenty-six. How long can he keep up his present pace? Already one hears mutterings from young men, tired of the older political parties, who look to him to lead them in a new political movement. Is his star to shine clearer and clearer, or is it to burn itself out by its very vehemence? Who can say?"

<u>Left:</u> **A cutting from** *Harper's Bazaar,* **1900**

<u>Opposite:</u> **Winston Churchill, 1900**
On 25 July 1900, five days after reaching England from South Africa, Churchill was again adopted as Conservative candidate for Oldham. Three days later he learned that his mother had married again: her new husband, George Cornwallis-West, was only 16 days older than he was.

<u>Below:</u> **Christmas card from the the Massey Music Hall in Canada advertising a talk by Churchill, 1900**
Churchill chose not to attend the opening of Parliament in December 1900. Instead he embarked on a speaking tour of Britain, the United States and Canada, recounting his wartime experiences. With the success of this tour and through his prolific writing in various journals and books, he earned £10,000 in 1899 and 1900, the equivalent of over a million pounds today. Members of Parliament at that time were unpaid and Churchill had inherited almost no money; the income he did receive from his father's estate, he assigned to his mother in 1903. He took his seat in Parliament in February 1901.

His maiden speech was an attack on his own party's proposal to increase British military expenditure. On 13 May 1901 he told the House of Commons: 'I have frequently been astonished since I have been in this House to hear with what composure and how glibly Members and even Ministers talk of a European war... a European war can only end in the ruin of the vanquished and the scarcely less fatal commercial dislocation and exhaustion of the conquerors.'

Winston later wrote to his brother Jack: 'I went to the House of Commons yesterday where I was treated with great civility by many people... I have greatly improved my position in England by the events of last year... The newspapers all give me paragraphs wherever I make a speech and a great many of the country newspapers write leading articles upon it.'

3

*Early
Political
Career:
1900–1914*

Churchill sailed from Cape Town and reached England on 20 July 1900. By this time, his vaulting political ambitions were already well understood by his contemporaries.

Drawing of Young Winston by Spy, published in *Vanity Fair*, 10 July 1900

While Churchill was still on his way home from South Africa, this illustration by the caricaturist Leslie Ward, working under the pseudonym Spy, was published in *Vanity Fair*.

The cartoon is strikingly similar to one of Winston's father drawn some 20 years previously by the same artist. The caption read: 'He is a clever fellow who has the courage of his opinions... He can write and he can fight... he has hankered after Politics since he was a small boy, and it is probable that his every effort, military or literary, has been made with political bent... He is something of a sportsman; who prides himself on being practical rather than a dandy; he is ambitious; he means to get on, and he loves his country. But he can hardly be the slave of any Party.'

Winston at Blenheim Palace with his American cousin by marriage, the Duchess of Marlborough, the former Consuelo Vanderbilt

The Duke of Marlborough, known to his intimates as 'Sunny', had married Consuelo Vanderbilt in 1895 in New York. It was the event of the year, with 300 policemen stationed outside the church to hold back the thousands of onlookers desperate to catch a glimpse of the glamorous bride.

However, it was a marriage of convenience and Consuelo came to the altar in tears, having been forced into the union by her mother. Her gown was very much her own choice, though: reportedly costing a staggering $6,720.35, it was cream satin with a pearl and silver embroidered train. She was a great beauty, of whom the playwright J. M. Barrie, author of *Peter Pan*, wrote: 'I would stand all day in the street to see Consuelo Marlborough get into her carriage.' After the dissolution of her marriage in 1921, Consuelo still maintained ties with Winston. In the 1920s and '30s, he was a frequent visitor to her château in Saint-Georges-Motel, some 50 miles from Paris. It was here that he completed his last painting before the war.

During 1903 and 1904, Winston often stayed at Blenheim, scouring the archives to write the biography of his father, for which the publishers paid him £8,000. Then, at a ball given by Lord and Lady Crewe in Mayfair in the early summer of 1904, he first met Clementine Hozier.

During the Imperial Army's manoeuvres in Breslau in 1906, Winston noted the Kaiser's restlessness: 'All he wished was to feel like Napoleon, and be like him, without having had to fight his battles.'

Winston with Kaiser Wilhelm II during the Imperial German Army's autumn manoeuvres, Breslau, 1906
In 1891, at the age of 17, Winston had seen the German Emperor in London. In a letter to his brother he described the Emperor's uniform: 'A helmet of bright Brass surmounted by a white eagle nearly 6 inches high. A Polished steel cuirass & a perfectly white uniform with high boots.'

In Breslau in 1906, he noted the Kaiser's restlessness: 'All he wished was to feel like Napoleon, and be like him, without having had to fight his battles'. He was invited to attend the army's manoeuvres again in 1909.

After the Great War, Winston wrote: 'No one should judge the career of the Emperor William II without asking the question, "What should I have done in his position?" Imagine yourself brought up from childhood to believe that you were appointed by God to be the ruler of a mighty nation, and that the inherent virtue of your blood raised you far above ordinary mortals... Imagine feeling the magnificent German race bounding beneath you in ever-swelling numbers, strength, wealth and ambition; and imagine on every side the thunderous tributes of crowd-loyalty and the skilled unceasing flattery of courtierly adulation... It is shocking to reflect that upon the word or nod of a being so limited there stood attentive and obedient for thirty years the forces which, whenever released, could devastate the world. It was not his fault; it was his fate.'

Churchill campaigns in Manchester, April 1908

In 1906, having disagreed with the Conservative Party on a variety of issues, Churchill stood as a Liberal candidate for Manchester North West and won. Under the regulations of the time, he had to seek re-election when, in 1908, he was appointed to the Cabinet as the President of the Board of Trade. He lost.

In the spring of 1908 he also met Clementine Hozier again. Their first meeting had been marred by his social awkwardness: she had felt uncomfortable with him just gazing at her, not saying a word. Now they were both guests of her great-aunt, Lady St Helier. Winston found to his delight that he was seated next to Clementine. Smitten by her beauty but, now more confident, he found her vivacious and intelligent. She was equally swept away by his brilliance and charm.

On 27 April 1908, three days after losing his seat in Manchester, he wrote to Clementine: 'I am glad to think you watched the battle from afar with eyes sympathetic to my fortune... Still I don't pretend not to be vexed. Defeat however consoled explained or discounted is odious... There is only one salve – everything in human power was done... Life for all its incompleteness is rather fun sometimes.'

Soon afterwards, he was elected at Dundee, a seat he was to hold for 14 years.

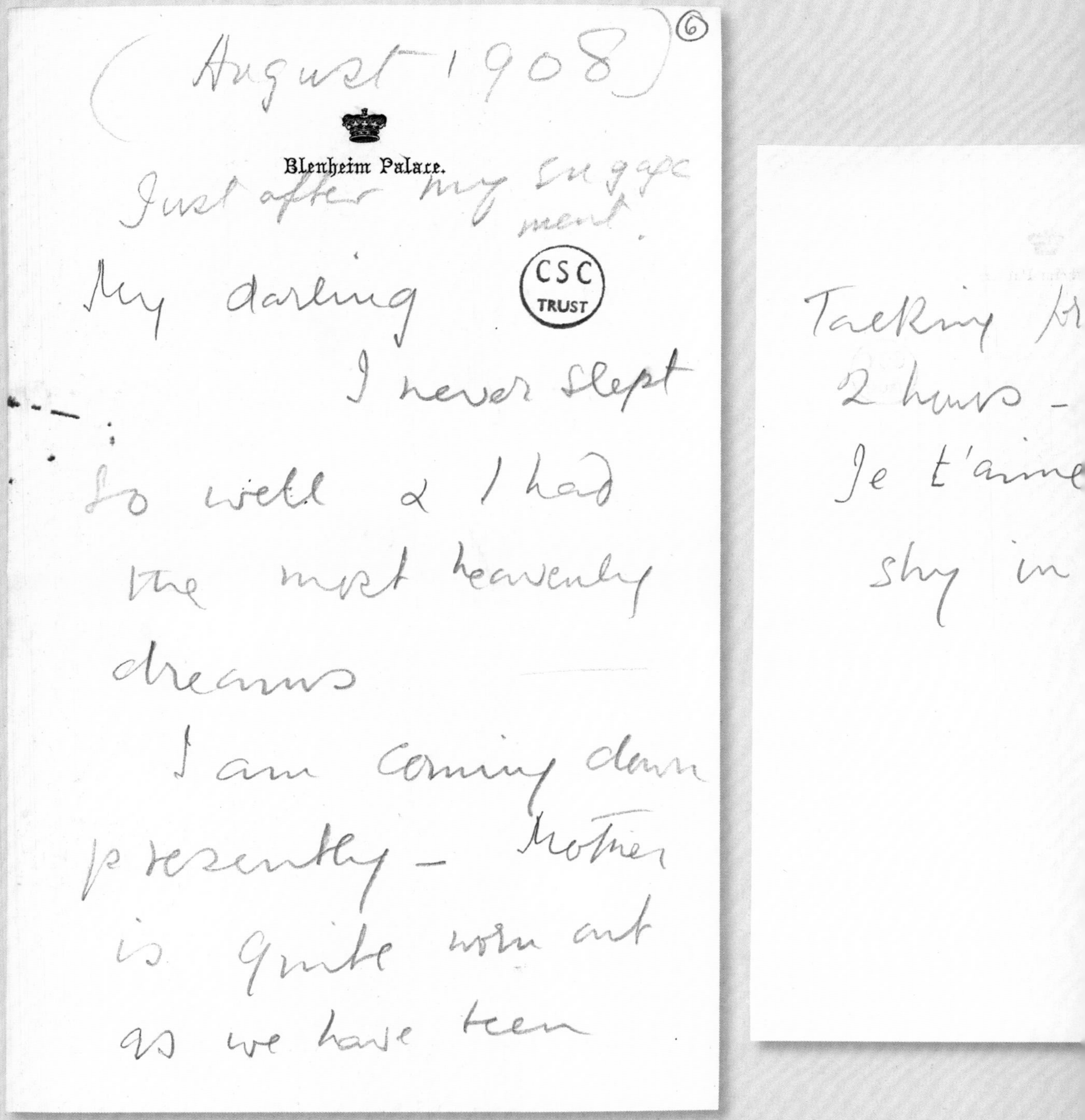

(August 1908) ⑥

Blenheim Palace.

Just after my engagement.

My darling

I never slept
so well & I had
the most heavenly
dreams

I am coming down
presently — Mother
is quite worn out
as we have been

Talking for
2 hours —
Je t'aime
shy in

Cart

ssionément – I feel less

nch

Clementine

Clementine's letter to Winston, 12 August 1908

During the summer of 1908, Winston and Clementine saw each other several times at social occasions. Pressing his suit, Winston invited her to Blenheim.

The house party assembled on 10 August and Winston arranged to walk with Clementine in the garden after breakfast the following day. She was characteristically punctual. Winston, as was his habit, remained in his bedroom late into the morning. His cousin, the Duke, gave him a piece of his mind: Winston would, if he wanted to marry Clementine, have to get himself out of bed, go down there and propose.

That afternoon, in the little Temple of Diana overlooking the great lake, Winston proposed and was accepted. The next day, he sent Clementine a note:

My dearest – I hope you have slept like a stone. I did not get to bed till 1 o'clock; for Sunny kept me long in discussion about his affairs wh. go less prosperously than ours. But from 1 onwards I slept the sleep of the just, & this morning am fresh & fit. Tell me how you feel & whether you mean to get up for breakfast. The purpose of this letter is also to send you heaps of love and four kisses
X X X X
From
Your always devoted
Winston

Clementine's reply, shown here, ends with the line 'Je t'aime passionement – I feel less shy in French.'

'At Blenheim I took two very important decisions: to be born and to marry,' Winston later wrote. 'I am happily content with the decisions I took on both those occasions.'

Secret till Sat.

41579

12 Aug 1908

12, BOLTON STREET,
W.

Pamela. I am going to marry Clementine & I say to you as you said to me when you married Victor – you must always be our best friend.

Ever yours

W.

Letter from Winston to Pamela Plowden, 12 August 1908

Winston had fallen in love with Pamela Plowden in Hyderabad in November 1896, and it was thought they were informally engaged.

'She is the most beautiful girl I have ever seen,' Winston wrote to his mother. She in turn wrote to him, 'Pamela is devoted to you and if yr love has grown as hers – I have no doubt it is only a question of time for you 2 marry.'

'I have lived all my life seeing the most beautiful women London produces,' Winston wrote to Pamela from Calcutta. 'Never have I seen one for whom I would forego the business of life. Then I met you... Were I a dreamer of dreams, I would say... "Marry me – and I will conquer the world and lay it at your feet." For marriage two conditions are necessary – money and the consent of both parties. One certainly, both probably are absent. And this is all such an old story...'

Pamela did not take up his grand offer and married Victor, Earl of Lytton, the son of the Viceroy of India, in April 1902. Winston wrote to her on 12 August 1908:

Pamela – I am going to marry Clementine & I say to you as you said to me when you married Victor – you must always be our best friend.

Ever yours, W.

Clementine and Winston, now engaged, 1908
Winston wrote to Clementine's mother on 12 August 1908:

My dear Lady Blanche Hozier,
Clementine will be my ambassador today. I have asked her to marry
me & we both ask you to give your consent & your blessing. You have
known my family for so many years that there is no need to say very
much in this letter. I am not rich nor powerfully established, but your
daughter loves me & with that love I feel strong enough to assume this
great & sacred responsibility; & I think I can make her happy & give
her a station & career worthy of her beauty and her virtues.

Marlborough is very much in hopes that you will be able to come
down here today & he is telegraphing to you this morning. That

would indeed be very charming & I am sure Clementine will
persuade you.

With sincere affection
Yours ever,
Winston S. Churchill

Once Lady Blanche's permission had been obtained, the engagement was announced, on 15 August on the court page of *The Times*.

'[M]arriage will be excellent for you mentally, morally & politically,' wrote Lord Hugh Cecil, Winston's best man. 'A bachelor is regarded as morally unprincipled.'

Churchill arrives in a taxi at Caxton Hall to obtain his marriage licence, September 1908

Winston's best man, Lord Hugh Cecil, had helpfully addressed the question of the marriage licence: 'I fancy the Brd of Trade will make you a resident in St Margaret's parish. But if not you shd take a room in the West Palace Hotel. After a fortnight's residence (I think) you can apply for an ordinary licence. A special licence costs a lot of money (£30?) so you had better go for an ordinary one or for banns.'

While Winston made the official arrangements, his fiancée was, in the company of her mother, busy shopping and seeing her dressmaker. A somewhat tired Clementine wrote to Winston that 'thinking about you has been the only pleasant thing today. I have tried on so many garments (all of which I am told are indispensable)...'

When news of the engagement reached Dieppe, where Clementine's family was well known, a fishwife who was a friend of the family ran through the streets crying: '*Ecoutez, écoutez! Voilà! La fille de la dame en bleu est fiancée avec un Anglais, ministre, millionaire, et decoré!*' ('Listen to this! The daughter of the lady in blue is engaged to a decorated English minister and millionaire!)

Opposite: *A Cabinet Minister's wedding*
Churchill's wedding to Clementine took place on 12 September 1908 at St Margaret's, Westminster, the parish church of the House of Commons.

The Bride Leaving Lady St. Helier's House

Where the reception was given

A CABINET MINISTER'S WEDDING.

Mr. Winston Churchill to Miss Clementine Hozier

At St. Margaret's, Westminster

Saturday Sept. 12, 1908

The Bride

The Crowd Outside St. Margaret's

On Saturday afternoon

The Bridegroom Arriving

Mr. Winston Churchill alighting at St. Margaret's, Westminster

Drawn by Wal Paget

The Marriage Ceremony in St. Margaret's, Westminster

The address to the newly-married couple was delivered by Bishop Welldon, who was formerly Mr. Winston Churchill's master at Harrow School. The honeymoon is being spent at Blenheim and at the Italian lakes

The Bride Arriving

With her brother, Sub-Lieutenant Hozier, at St. Margaret's

Two of the Bridesmaids

Miss Madeline Whyte on the left and Miss Claire Frewen on the right

After the Wedding

The bride and bridegroom

The Bride's Brother

Sub-Lieutenant Hozier

Friends after the Battle

Mr. and Mrs. Joynson-Hicks

A Distinguished Guest

The Duchess of Marlborough at the wedding

The marriage of Winston and Clementine Churchill was described by the *Daily Mirror* as 'the most popular and interesting wedding of the year'.

Letter from Winston to his mother, written from Blenheim Palace on 13 September 1908, the day after his marriage to Clementine

Dearest Mamma
Everything is comfortable & satisfactory in every way down here, & Clemmie happy & beautiful. The weather is a little austere with gleams of sunshine; we shall long for warm Italian suns. There was no need for any anxiety. She tells me she is writing you a letter. Best of love my dearest Mamma, you are a great comfort & support to me at a critical period in my emotional development. We have never been so much together so often in a short time. God bless you.
    What a relief to have got that ceremony over! & so happily.
    Your loving son,
    W.

P.S. I open this letter again to tell you that George [Lady Randolph's second husband] said he could wish me no better wife or happier days than he had found in you.

At the wedding, James Welldon, Winston's headmaster at Harrow and now Bishop Welldon, had said in his address: 'There must be in the statesman's life many times when he depends upon the love, the insight, the penetrating sympathy, and devotion of his wife. The influence which the wives of our statesmen have exercised for good upon their husbands' lives is an unwritten chapter of English history, too sacred perhaps to be written in full.'

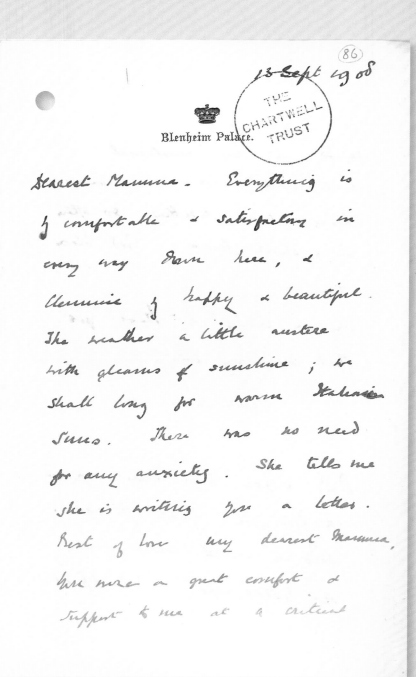

period in my emotional
development. We have never
been so much together so often
in a short time. God bless
you.
What a relief to have got
that ceremony over! & so happily

  Your loving son

    W.

P.S. I open this letter again
& tell you that George
said he could wish me
no better wife & happier

days there he had formed
in you.

The wedding was covered extensively in the press. 'Not for many years has a marriage excited such widespread interest,' the *Scotsman* wrote. *The New York Times* devoted two columns to the event, and in the list of gifts noted: 'Winston Churchill is an author, and an inkpot is an appropriate present for him. But what author can make use of twenty-two inkpots...'

Among the other wedding gifts was a gold-headed walking-stick from King Edward VII, which Winston was to use for the rest of his life. He also received a ten-volume edition of Jane Austen's collected works from the Prime Minister. Volume three contains the first part of *Pride and Prejudice* and is inscribed to Winston: 'H. H. Asquith 12 September 1908 *nec aspera terrent.*' ('Difficulties be damned').

The Chancellor of the Exchequer Lloyd George wrote of the union: 'Your luck has followed you into the most important transaction of your life.' He was also among those who signed the register.

During his two years at the Board of Trade, Churchill was a strong advocate of state aid to the sick and the unemployed. He also set up a number of Labour Exchanges to help the unemployed find work.

Winston and Clementine visit the Whitehall Labour Exchange, 1 February 1910

On 1 February 1910, Churchill and his wife visited a Labour Exchange in Whitehall, one of 17 opened that day. Nearly two years earlier, on 14 March 1908, Churchill had written to Asquith: 'Dimly across gulfs of ignorance I see the outline of a policy wh I call the Minimum Standard... Underneath, though not in substitution for, the immense disjoined fabric of social safeguards & insurances which has grown up by itself in England, there must be spread – at a lower level – a sort of Germanised network of State intervention & regulation.'

On 8 January 1910, Churchill spoke in Asquith's East Fife constituency to defend the social reforms of the Liberal government:

'In the centre of this scheme stands the great principle of national insurance against unemployment, invalidity, sickness, infirmity and the death of the breadwinner. This is linked with the system of national labour exchanges, now being established, and with large projects for reforming the Poor Law, for rescuing children from the workhouse, for providing for the proper treatment of the feeble-minded, for inebriates, and others in places specially suited for their care, and for discriminating between the honest worker in search of a job and the idle loafer in search of a tip.'

Mrs Lloyd George, Lloyd George, Churchill and William Clark, Lloyd George's secretary, on the way to the House of Commons for the Chancellor's Budget, 27 April 1910
Churchill wanted strong measures should the Lords reject Lloyd George's controversial Budget. 'The time has come for the total abolition of the House of Lords,' he wrote to Asquith on 14 February 1910. On 31 March, the government introduced proposals to curb the power of the Lords. Churchill spoke for the Bill: 'We have reached a fateful period in British history. The time for words is past; the time for action has arrived. Since the House of Lords, upon an evil and unpatriotic instigation – as I must judge it – have used their Veto to affront the Prerogative of the Crown and to invade the rights of the Commons, it has now become necessary that the Crown and the Commons, acting together, should restore the balance of the Constitution and restrict for ever the Veto of the House of Lords.'

However, the Budget passed the Commons by 324 votes to 231 and the Lords agreed to it without a division. That evening, Churchill wrote to Edward VII: 'Everyone is tired out by the unceasing strain, and the holiday of a month is the dearest wish of most Members of the House of Commons.' Soon after, on 6 May, the King died.

The back of 100 Sidney Street, London, where
two armed anarchists were trapped and killed,
3 January 1911

In January 1911, armed policemen and a platoon of
riflemen from the Scots Guards laid siege to a house
in London's East End in which a gang of suspected
anarchists of Latvian extraction had taken refuge.
Having been interrupted when tunnelling into a
jeweller's shop in Houndsditch, the gang had shot and
killed three policemen attempting to apprehend them
before fleeing to the house at 100 Sidney Street.

Churchill is believed to have been in the bath at
his home in Eccleston Square, Pimlico, when he
received news of the confrontation in the East End.
He immediately made it his business to attend the
scene, and photographs of him subsequently appeared
in the press, a striking figure in a top hat and an
astrakhan-collared overcoat as he took charge of the
situation. Despite the bullets flying from the house,
Winston remained calm. He dissuaded police officers
from putting their lives in danger by storming the
premises and also instructed the fire brigade not to
risk intervening when fire broke out and destroyed
the house. The remains of two bodies were found
inside, but an unknown number of other members of
the gang, including their leader, known as Peter the
Painter, escaped and were never found.

Later that day Churchill wrote to the Prime
Minister, Herbert Asquith: 'It was a striking scene in
a London street – firing from every window, bullets
chipping the brickwork, police and Scots Guards
armed with loaded weapons artillery brought up...
I thought it better to let the House burn than spend
good British lives in rescuing those ferocious rascals.'

Churchill giving evidence at the Sidney Street inquest,
18 January 1911

A week after the siege at Sidney Street, Churchill recalled:
'I made it my business, however, after seeing what was going
on in front to go around the back of the premises and satisfy
myself that there was no chance of the criminals effecting
their escape through the intricate area of walls and small
houses at the back of No 100 Sidney Street. This took some
time, and when I returned to the corner of Sidney Street
I was told that the house had caught on fire, and I could see
smoke coming out from the top-floor window.'

After the fire had burnt itself out the police entered the
building and found two bodies. One of the men had been
shot, the other had died of asphyxiation.

To some, the incident confirmed Churchill's reputation
as a man of action, but to others his behaviour appeared
foolhardy. He was criticized in the press for having
conducted the operation and for giving orders to the police
and firemen.

Front cover of the record of the
Houndsditch Murders Inquest, 1911

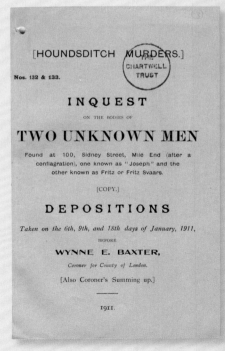

[HOUNDSDITCH MURDERS.]

[CHARTWELL TRUST]

Nos. 132 & 133.

INQUEST

ON THE BODIES OF

TWO UNKNOWN MEN

Found at 100, Sidney Street, Mile End (after a
conflagration), one known as "Joseph" and the
other known as Fritz or Fritz Svaars.

[COPY.]

DEPOSITIONS

Taken on the 6th, 9th, and 18th days of January, 1911,

BEFORE

WYNNE E. BAXTER,

Coroner for County of London.

[Also Coroner's Summing up.]

1911.

WINSTON LEONARD SPENCER CHURCHILL, UPON HIS OATH SAITH :

(*Examined* 18*th January*, 1911).

I am Privy Councillor and Principal Secretary of State for the Home Department.

On Tuesday, 3rd January, I received a message from the Home Office about 11 a.m. that the War Office was enquiring if authority could be given for 20 men of the Scots Guards to proceed to the aid of the police in Stepney. The message stated that the criminals believed to be implicated in the Houndsditch murders had been located and that they were firing on the police, and that one police officer had been mortally wounded. I communicated with my advisers at the Home Office on the telephone, and gave the authority that was asked. I was at my house when I got the message. Then I went on to the Home Office and tried to get more information. I could get no more information by telephoning, except that there was a regular fusilade going on in Stepney. I could get no definite or exact information of what was happening. In my opinion the circumstances were extraordinary, and I thought it my duty to go and see for

---

Transcript of Churchill's evidence
from the Inquest Report,
18 January 1911

Sydney Holland, later Viscount Knutsford, who was with Churchill throughout the siege, wrote to him before the inquest: 'The only possible excuse for anyone saying that you gave orders is that you did once and very rightly go forward and wave back the crowd at the far end of the road. If those miscreants had come out there would have been lots of people shot by soldiers. And you did also give orders that you and I were not to be shot in our hindquarters by a policeman who was standing with a 12 bore behind you!'

Churchill stated at the inquest: 'I never directed anyone to send for a Maxim gun, nor did I send at any time for further military force.' Reflecting on the events at Sidney Street 13 years later, he wrote: 'No one knew how many Anarchists there were or what measures were going to be taken. In these circumstances I thought it my duty to see what was going on myself... I must, however, admit that convictions of duty were supported by a strong sense of curiosity which perhaps it would have been as well to keep in check.'

myself what was happening. I went in a motor car to Sidney Street. I reached there about 11.50 a.m. When I got there I heard that some Scots Guards had been there long before I received any application at all.

My sanction was not legally necessary. When I got to Sidney Street I enquired who was the Senior Officer in command. I was told that Major Wodehouse was so, but that he had gone to the War Office a few minutes before I arrived, and that Superintendent Mulvaney was in charge of the Metropolitan Police. I saw Mr. Mulvaney and others, and when I got there firing was going on there from the house. There were crowds at all the approaches and police officers were keeping them away. I saw a few soldiers. I remained there, and a little before 1 p.m. it was noticed that smoke was coming from the premises. At that time firing was still proceeding at and from the house. At about 1.5 p.m. some representatives of the Fire Brigade arrived with their appliances. A junior officer of the Fire Brigade (Station Officer Edmonds) came up to me where I was standing and said that the Fire Brigade had arrived, and that he understood he was not to put out the fire at present. Was this right ? or words to that effect. I said, " Quite right ; I accept full responsibility." I wish to make it clear that these words refer to the specific question asked me, and that I confirmed and supported the police in their action. From what I saw, it would have meant loss of life and limb to any fire brigade officer who had gone within effective range of the building. Assistant Divisional Officer Morris, of the Fire Brigade, was there, and I asked him whether he could be sure of getting the fire under when it became safe for the men to advance. He said he was making all preparations with the hosery, but that for greater precaution he would order up 4 more steamers. I was there when the Brigade were able to go to the fire. I left about 2.40 or 2.45 p.m. I did not see Major Wodehouse on the scene at any time that day to my recollection. I did not in any way direct or override the arrangements that the police authorities had made. I gave no directions to alter arrangements already made by them. I suggested the crowd being moved back beyond the line of fire. I think I did so to Mr. Mulvaney. It would be quite untrue to say that I took the direction out of the hands of the Executive Officers. I did not in any way interfere with the arrangements made by the police. I was only there to support them in any unusual difficulty as a covering authority.

So far as I am concerned, the police had a free hand. I heard that a Maxim gun had arrived (from persons around me). I never directed anyone to send for a Maxim gun, nor did I send at any time for any further military force. The artillery came up as I was driving away. I met them. I should like to put on record that among the police and plain clothes officers all round the building there was a general and perfect readiness to volunteer to rush the building at any moment, and that any

Churchill was an eager advocate of flying. As early as February 1909, he had told the Aerial Navigation Sub-Committee of the Committee of Imperial Defence that the issue of aeroplanes 'was a most important one'.

Churchill and Lord Northcliffe at the Hendon Aviation Meeting, 12 May 1911

At Hendon, Churchill watched the aviator Claude Grahame-White drop a bomb on an area marked out to resemble the deck of a ship. The demonstration was organized by the Parliamentary Aerial Defence Committee. Winston is seen here talking to Lord Northcliffe, the owner of the *Daily Mail*, who was an early exponent of the view that Germany was a serious military threat to Britain and firmly believed in harnessing the nascent power of aviation to combat this threat.

On 24 October 1911, Churchill became First Lord of the Admiralty. He built up the Royal Naval Air Service and was encouraged in his decision by Admiral of the Fleet Lord Fisher. More than two years earlier Churchill had attended an Army Field Day in Berkshire. In a letter to Clementine he wrote: 'These military men vy often fail altogether to see the simple truths underlying the relationships of all armed forces, & how the levers of power can be used upon them. Do you know I would greatly like to have some practice in the handling of large forces. I have much confidence in my judgement on things, when I see clearly, but on nothing do I seem to feel the truth more than in tactical combinations. It is a vain and foolish thing to say – but you will not laugh at it. I am sure I have the root of the matter in me...'

Winston and his mother (aged 55), 1911

In the summer of 1900, Lady Randolph had married George Cornwallis-West; she was 46, he 26, a mere 16 days older than Winston. They divorced in 1913, after he left her for the celebrated actress Mrs Patrick Campbell. In the summer of 1918, Jennie married Montagu Porch, of the North Nigerian Civil Service. She was 63, he 40, three years younger than Winston: 'Not unnaturally, this event was the cause of mixed feelings among Jennie's relations – including a degree of embarrassment.'

Jennie died in June 1921. Churchill later wrote to Lord Curzon, the Foreign Secretary: 'I do not feel a sense of tragedy, but only of loss. Her life was a full one. The wine of life was in her veins. Sorrows and storms were conquered by her nature & on the whole it was a life of sunshine.

'My mother always seemed to me a fairy princess: a radiant being possessed of limitless riches and power.' In advancing his career, Winston wrote in *My Early Life*, 'she cooperated energetically from her end. In my interest she left no wire unpulled, no stone unturned, no cutlet uncooked.'

Winston and Clementine Churchill pictured on the cover of *Tatler* **magazine, 11 October 1911**

Winston and his wife appeared in their swimming costumes on the cover of society magazine *Tatler* in October 1911: the 36-year-old politician is shown frolicking in the waves and lazing on a canoe with Clementine and their friend Captain Jervis as they holidayed in Dieppe. Under the headline 'Catching Winston Unbending', *Tatler* noted that the Churchills were enjoying themselves 'far from the madding crowd's ignoble strife'.

Winston enjoyed seaside holidays and spent hours making elaborate castles and forts in the sand. '[W]e ought to find a really good sandy beach,' he wrote to Clementine, 'where I can cut the sand into a nicely bevelled fortress – or best of all with a little stream running down.'

This echoes the memories of Sir Shane Leslie, Winston's cousin: 'I have a photograph of a group taken in Brighton in 1889... our great employment there was being drilled in Winston's army. There was some eight of us and the gardeners' boys. It was an army that never changed its commander and for the ranks there was no promotion. We dug and built a mud fortification we called "The Den" [with a] drawbridge over the moat. There we sat in perfect happiness and much mud, "waiting", as Winston said, for the enemies of England. We really had to wait fifty years, but we were ready.'

The TATLER

Vol. XLII. No. 537.
London, October 11, 1911

REGISTERED AT THE GENERAL POST OFFICE AS A NEWSPAPER Sixpence.

CATCHING WINSTON UNBENDING

Our top picture depicts Mr. and Mrs. Winston Churchill with Captain Jervis disporting themselves in a double canoe at Dieppe, where the Home Secretary has recently been holidaying. The lower picture shows Mr. Churchill being rocked in the cradle of the deep—deep to deep—with his wife in the background. A further picture of this eminent statesman is shown on a subsequent page

31

Winston and Clementine 'playing bears' with their one-year-old son, Randolph, summer 1912

The arrival of first one child, Diana (born 11 July 1909), and then another, Randolph (born 28 May 1911 and nicknamed 'Chumbolly'), only seemed to bring Churchill and his wife closer together. On 4 June 1911, Clementine wrote to her husband: 'The Chumbolly & I are both very well. It is a lovely calm evening after a most sultry airless day & I have been thinking of you with pleasure among the green trees & cool waters... I am so happy with you my Dear. You have so transformed my life that I can hardly remember what it felt like three years ago before I knew you.'

On 23 July 1913 Winston wrote to her, from the Admiralty yacht HMS *Enchantress*: 'Tender love to you my sweet one & to both those little kittens & especially that radiant Randolph. Diana is a darling too: & I repent to have expressed a preference. But somehow he seems a more genial generous nature: while she is mysterious and self-conscious.'

On 2 November 1913, Clementine wrote to Winston that 'I found two delicious slumbering kittens, Randolph with his little arms flung out over his head looking like a sweet cherub.' The following April, when Clementine had been away, Winston wrote: 'I asked Randolph this morning whether he wanted you to come back & why & he said "Becos I lurve her".'

Churchill saw his prime task as First Lord of the Admiralty to expand the British navy in the North Sea, to compete against the rise of the ever-menacing German High Seas Fleet.

Churchill and his mother on board a replica of Drake's galleon *Revenge*, Earl's Court, July 1912

In May 1912, Churchill's mother produced an exhibition at Earl's Court in London entitled 'Shakespeare's England', the centrepiece of which was a replica of Sir Francis Drake's ship, the *Revenge*. The exhibition was not a financial success. 'Fiasco at Earl's Court,' wrote *The New York Times* on 4 August, asserting that 'the show has been an unmitigated failure'.

Winston, as First Lord of the Admiralty, visited the exhibition in July and made a speech, reported in *The Times* on the 22nd, in which he talked about 'the greatest traditions of the British Fleet' and described the *Revenge* as 'one of the most historic vessels on which the glories of the British Navy had depended'.

**Winston and Clementine after the launch of
the dreadnought battleship *Iron Duke*, Portsmouth,
October 1912**

Churchill suggested to King George V that a dreadnought
to be launched in October 1912 should be named HMS
Iron Duke, as a more evocative alternative to the original
suggestion, *Wellington*.

In July 1912, speaking to the House of Commons, Winston
had declared that 'the state of Europe and of the world would
seem to contain many more germs of danger than the period
through which we have been passing in our lifetime'. He
stated that there were two general principles: 'First that we
must have an ample margin of strength instantly ready;
and, secondly, that there must be a steady and systematic

development of our naval forces untiringly pursued over a
number of years.'

In a 1909 speech, Lloyd George had famously quipped
that 'a fully equipped Duke costs as much to keep up as two
Dreadnoughts, and Dukes are just as great a terror, and they
last longer.'

HMS *Iron Duke* became flagship of the Grand Fleet and
saw action at Jutland in 1916, inflicting damage on the
German battleship *König*. Able Seaman Arthur Sawyer,
who was aboard the *Iron Duke* during the battle, recalled
that 'when the five turrets fired at the same time, the ship
just stood still and shook... we did hear that our 13.5-inch
guns had scored seven hits on the *König*'.

At Bristol Station, on Saturday, a frantic suffragist attacked Mr. Winston Churchill with a dog whip.

O, Woman, in our hours of ease
Uncertain, coy, and hard to please.

When pain and anguish wring the brow,
A ministering angel thou!

Cartoon of Churchill being attacked by a suffragette, *Manchester Evening News*, 1909

An early example of 'Suffragette Outrage' occurred on 20 November 1909, when Theresa Garnett attacked Churchill with a dog whip on the platform of Bristol Temple Meads station. He had just stepped off a train when Miss Garnett brandished the whip and struck him, screaming: 'Take that in the name of the insulted women of England!' Fortunately for Churchill, his hat protected his head.

As detectives led Miss Garnett away she called out to him: 'You brute, why don't you treat British women properly?' She was arrested for assault, but Churchill did not press charges, as he did not want to appear in court; Miss Garnett ended up with a one-month prison sentence for disturbing the peace and was force-fed during her time in Horfield Prison.

Shortly after this incident, Churchill received a deputation of suffragettes, to whom he said: 'I am bound to say I think your cause has marched backwards.' However, the prominent suffragette Christabel Pankhurst wrote: 'Moved by the spirit of pure chivalry, Miss Garnett took what she thought to be the best available means of avenging the insult done to womanhood by the Government to which Mr. Churchill belongs.'

In 1913 an unsuccessful attempt was made by suffragettes to kidnap the young Randolph from his pram.

Churchill is harassed by a suffragette in Aberdeen, in a photograph published in *Votes for Women*, 13 September 1912
'I do not wish to be committed at the present juncture to any special form or basis in or upon which the franchise is to be granted to women,' Churchill wrote in April 1910. 'I am, however, anxious to see women relieved in principle from a disability which is injurious to them whilst it is based on grounds of sex.'

For throwing a potato at Churchill's window, Katherine Willoughby Marshall was imprisoned for two weeks in December 1910. 'The potato was well wrapped with various messages about our having justice,' she recalled. 'I chose a potato because my husband objected to my throwing a stone, in case I hurt anybody.'

Violet Bonham Carter (daughter of Prime Minister H. H. Asquith and a close friend of Churchill's) felt that his 'approach to women was essentially romantic'. She thought that 'he divided women into two categories – the virginal snowdrops, unsullied by experience, or even knowledge, of the seamy side of life, who should be sheltered and protected from its hazards; and the mature who were at home among the seams, had scrambled in and out of pitfalls and adventures and to whom he could talk without protective inhibitions in his own language'.

Churchill in the cockpit, having a flying lesson with Captain Wildman-Lushington RM, probably at Eastchurch Airfield, Kent, 1913

In 1912 Churchill made his first flight in an aeroplane and in 1913 he started to learn to fly himself. After a practice on 23 October, he wrote to Clementine: 'It has been as good as one of those old days in the S. African war, & I have lived entirely in the moment, with no care for all those tiresome party politics & searching newspapers, & awkward by-elections... For good luck before I started I put your locket on.'

Churchill's flying instructor Gilbert Wildman-Lushington wrote to his fiancée Airlie Hynes in November 1913: 'I started Winston off in his instruction about 12.15 and he got so bitten with it, I could hardly get him out of the machine.' Unfortunately, Wildman-Lushington crashed

on landing three days later and was killed. His fiancée later wrote to Churchill: 'He was so pleased at having given you your first instruction, and his last letters were all about it and he was so happy.'

On 29 May 1914, Churchill wrote to his wife from Portsmouth: 'My darling one, I have been at the Central Flying School for a couple of days – flying a little in good & careful hands & under perfect conditions. So I did not write you from there as I know you wd be vexed.' In her letter of 5 June, Clementine wrote: '[E]very time I see a telegram now, I think it is to announce that you have been killed.' He acknowledged her distress and wrote to her on 6 June: 'I will not fly any more... it was an important part of my life during the last 7 months, & I am sure my nerve, my spirits & my virtue were all improved by it. But at your expense my poor pussy cat! I am so sorry.'

Churchill and Colonel Jack Seely, the Secretary of State for War, aboard a naval vessel

Jack Seely was a great friend of Winston's. He was Secretary of State for War for the two years prior to the Great War, before being forced to resign as a result of the Curragh Incident in Ireland, which involved a near-revolt of British troops in Dublin and caused great embarrassment to Asquith's government. In March 1918, at the Battle of Moreuil Wood, Seely led one of the last cavalry charges in history on his horse, Warrior. He was the only former cabinet minister to go to the front in 1914 and still be there four years later.

Of his first encounter with Winston while both of them were at Harrow, Seely said: 'He really hated much of the school curriculum; it seemed to him such a shocking waste to spend so much time on dead languages and so little on his native tongue. I remember the Headmaster, Welldon, told me that it was an extraordinary thing to see in a boy of fourteen; I think his exact words were, "such a love and veneration for the English language".

'While other people, and even masters who were teaching him literature, could remember a line or two of a Shakespearian play, young Winston could quote whole scenes straight off; nor was he slow to take advantage of his remarkable gift of memory. If a master, however imposing, quoted a passage wrongly, Winston would instantly correct him. He was a most intrepid pupil...'

> Churchill is credited with saying that playing golf is 'like chasing a quinine pill around a cow pasture'.

Churchill playing golf in Cannes, probably as a guest of the actress Maxine Elliott, February 1913 Winston's son Randolph described the shot shown here thus: '[H]e fails to keep his head down and foozles his drive.' His daughter Mary was to say of her parents' sporting abilities:

'Clementine was generally energetic and athletic, greatly enjoying not only riding but also tennis and golf. Winston also played golf occasionally – but polo was really his game.'

As Home Secretary, Winston was a member of the Coombe Hill Golf Club, occasionally playing with Asquith.

His papers include the following entry: 'Played golf better this afternoon and slept 10 hours last night. We shall be up all night and I am going to put the screws on the Parliament Bill.'

Winston wrote to Clementine from Sussex in June 1911 that 'it has been a vy windy day but we have played

2 rounds of golf notwithstanding'. Accompanying him was Louis Botha (by now Prime Minister of the Union of South Africa), who had been Commander-in-Chief of the Boer forces during the war in which Winston had fought against him. In fact, Winston incorrectly believed Botha to have captured him at the ambush of a British armoured train on 15 November 1899.

Clementine taking part in the Ladies' Parliamentary Golf Tournament at Ranelagh, 1913

General Sir Ian Hamilton, Winston Churchill, his brother Jack Churchill and Winston's close friend the Conservative MP F. E. Smith attend army manoeuvres, Buckinghamshire, 1913

In September 1913 the British Army was involved in manoeuvres in the North Buckinghamshire countryside. Men of the 9th Division with cavalry advanced from the Chiltern Hills towards Daventry, across the county boundary in Northamptonshire.

Winston is seen here with General Sir Ian Hamilton. The two men first met when Churchill was a young soldier, and both would later be blamed for the failure of the Dardanelles campaign in 1915. In *Ian Hamilton's March*, published in 1900, Winston wrote that Hamilton had 'a fine taste in words, and an acute perception of the curious which he has preserved from his literary days... His mind is built upon a big scale, being broad and strong, capable of thinking in army corps and if necessary in continents, and working always with serene smoothness undisturbed alike by responsibility or danger.'

Of his friend F. E. Smith (later the Earl of Birkenhead), godfather to Randolph, Winston wrote, '[O]ur friendship was perfect. It was one of my most precious possessions. It was never marred by the slightest personal difference or misunderstanding... never did I separate from him without having learnt something, and enjoyed myself besides.'

4

*The
First
World War:
1914–1918*

In the first weeks of August 1914, 80,000 troops of the British Expeditionary Force (BEF) commanded by Field Marshal Sir John French landed in France.

Winston and Clementine Churchill on their way to the Houses of Parliament, 2 September 1914

Part of Field Marshal French's plan in August 1914 was to meet up with the French 5th Army near Charleroi in Belgium. Before reaching Charleroi, however, the BEF encountered cavalry patrols from the German 1st Army at the town of Soignies on 22 August. The next day the German 1st Army launched a frontal attack amid the slagheaps and pitheads of the coalfields of Mons. Realizing that they were up against a much greater force, the BEF gave the German troops a bloody nose before withdrawing to the Marne.

French wanted complete withdrawal to the coast but Field Marshal Herbert Kitchener, the new Secretary of State for War, rejected this suggestion, wanting the BEF to remain in contact with the French forces, also retreating to the Marne. An unhappy Sir John French informed the Cabinet that he no longer intended to co-operate with the French army.

Back in London, on 2 September, Churchill wrote to French: 'I have wanted so much to write to you ... a few lines from a friend. The Cabinet was bewildered by your telegram proposing to retire from the line... we feared that you and Joffre [Commander-in-Chief of the French forces] might have quarrelled, or that something had happened to the Army of which we had not been informed... I am only anxious that you shall be sustained and reinforced in every way.'

Private   May 14. 15

My dear Prime Minister,

I must ask you to take note of Fisher's statement today "that he was against the D⁷⁷ˢ & had been all along", or words to that effect. The 1SL has agreed in writing to every executive tel⁷ on wh the operations have been conducted; & had they been immediately successful, the credit wd have been his. But I make no complaint of that. I am attached to the old boy & it is a great pleasure to me to work with him. I think he reciprocates these feelings. My point is that a moment will probably arise in these operations when the Adl & Senⁱᵐ on the spot will wish & require to run a risk with the Fleet for a great & decisive effort. If I agree with them, I shall sanction it, &

I cannot undertake to be paralyzed by the veto of a friend who whatever the result will certainly say "I was always against the D⁷⁷ˢ". You will see that in a matter of this kind someone has to take the responsibility. I will do so — provided that my decision is the one that rules — & not otherwise.

It is also uncomfortable not to know what Kitchener will or wont do in the matter of reinforcements. We are absolutely in his hands, & I never saw him in a queerer mood — or more unreasonable. K. will punish the Admⁱʸ by docking Hamilton of his division, because we have withdrawn the Q. Elizⁿ; & Fisher will have the Q. Elizⁿ home if he is to stay.

Through all this with patience &

determination we can make our way to one of the great events in the history of the world.

But I wish now to make it clear to you that a man who says "I disclaim responsibility for failure" cannot be the final arbiter of the measure wh may be found to be vital to success.

This requires no answer. & I am quite contented with the course of affairs.

Yours always.
W.

I cannot undertake to be paralyzed by the veto of a friend who whatever the result will certainly say "I was always against the D⁷⁷ˢ".

Letter from Churchill to Asquith, 14 May 1915

Churchill had given much thought to his plan to take the Dardanelles. With the stalemate on the Western Front, he thought it would create another front that would force the Germans to support the Turkish army. A naval attack would be made in the narrow straits at the entrance to the Black Sea before the landing of troops. As well as splitting the German forces, the move would, if successful, enable the British to capture Constantinople (now Istanbul), the capital of the Ottoman Empire, and secure trading routes with Russia.

On 25 April 1915, Allied troops landed on the Gallipoli Peninsula in Turkey, but a well-entrenched, tenacious Turkish defence kept them at bay. The First Sea Lord, Admiral Fisher, who had formerly supported the campaign, now argued that it be abandoned. On 14 May he stated to the War Council that he had been against the Dardanelles operation from the beginning.

Churchill wrote to the Prime Minister: 'I must ask you to take note of Fisher's statement today that he was against the [Dardanelles] and had been all along... The First Sea Lord has agreed in writing to every executive telegram on which the operations have been conducted; & had they been immediately successful, the credit wd have been his.' On 15 May, Fisher resigned and Asquith determined to form a Coalition government. Churchill wrote to Asquith: 'Above all things I should like to stay here and complete my work, the most difficult part of which is ended.'

Churchill's hopes of staying in office after the
failed Dardanelles operation were in vain, and he
was replaced as First Lord of the Admiralty by
A. J. Balfour, the former Conservative Prime Minister.

**Churchill crossing Horse
Guards Parade with A. J. Balfour,
July 1915**

On 23 May 1915, Churchill was offered
the post of Chancellor of the Duchy of
Lancaster. Feeling demoted, he wrote
later: 'Like a sea-beast fished up from
the depths or a diver too suddenly
hoisted, my veins threatened to burst
from the fall in pressure.'

On 26 May, Churchill wrote to
A. J. Balfour, his successor as First
Lord of the Admiralty, about the
future of the Gallipoli campaign:
'The military operations shd proceed
with all possible speed so that the
period of danger may be shortened.
Whatever force is necessary, can be
spared, and can be used, shd be sent at
once, & all at once... Punishment must
be doggedly borne.'

In July, Kitchener asked Churchill
to go to the Dardanelles to assess the
situation. Winston never made this
journey, but he wrote to his wife on
17 July, expecting to come under fire
(he marked the envelope 'to be sent
to Mrs Churchill in the event of my
death'): 'Do not grieve for me too
much. I am a spirit confident of my
rights. Death is only an incident, & not
the most important wh happens to us
in this state of being. On the whole,
especially since I met you my darling
one I have been happy, & you have
taught me how noble a woman's heart
can be. If there is anywhere else I shall
be on the look out for you. Meanwhile
look forward, feel free, rejoice in
Life, cherish the children, guard my
memory. God bless you.'

Winston Churchill addresses a meeting at Enfield Munition Works (Clementine Churchill is seated on the left), 18 September 1915
Churchill spoke, at his wife's request, at Enfield Lock munitions works, where Clementine had established one of a number of canteens on behalf of the YMCA. He spoke twice, first to the men about to go on the night shift, and then to the men coming off the day shift:

'Our situation is a serious one. We have it in our power by our exertions to carry this war to a successful and a decisive conclusion, but we have it in our power to do so only if we exert our strength to the utmost limit of human and national capacity.

'After all we did not seek this struggle. We did not desire as a nation, or as a generation, to have imposed upon us this terrible ordeal...But we know that if in this time of crisis and strain we do our duty, we shall have done all that is in human power to do... whatever part we play on the stage of the world's history – we shall bear ourselves so that those who come after us will find amid the signs and scars of this great struggle that the liberties of Europe and of Britain are still intact and inviolate...I cannot but express most sincerely my gratitude for all the exertions which are being made, and I earnestly trust you will not flag or slacken in these, so that by your efforts our country may emerge from this period of darkness and peril once more into the sunlight of a peaceful time.'

23. XI. 15

My darling, we have finished our first 48 hours in the trenches & are now resting in billets in support...

Letter from Winston to Clementine, 23 November 1915

On 18 November 1915, Churchill left London for the Western Front, as a Major in the Queen's Own Oxfordshire Hussars. On his arrival, he wrote to Clementine: 'I am staying tonight at GHQ in a fine chateau, with hot baths, beds, champagne and all the conveniences... I am absolutely right to leave the Govt. They are descending into the abyss. I am sure I am going to be entirely happy out here & at peace. I must try to win my way as a good & sincere soldier. But do not suppose I shall run any foolish risks or do anything wh is not obviously required.'

On 23 November he wrote to her from Bout Deville (see left):

My darling, we have finished our first 48 hours in the trenches & are now resting in billets in support. We are near enough to hear rifle fire but out of range of everything except the artillery, wh will not be likely to bother about the cottages & farms in wh we are living. I have spent the morning on my toilet & a hot bath, engineered with some difficulty...I have lost all interest in the outer world and no longer worry about it or its stupid newspapers. I am living with the battalion H.qrters- Colonel, 2nd in command, adjutant. When the battalion is in the trenches we live about 1000 yards behind in a dugout in rear of a shattered farm. I spent Saturday night in the trenches instead – with Griggs' company: & when we go in again tomorrow night I am going to stay with them for the whole period. This gives me the opportunity of seeing & learning thoroughly.'

During his time at the Western Front, Churchill's eminent background in British public affairs enabled him to mingle on equal terms with higher-ranking officers.

Churchill at the French front line on 5 December 1915 with Captain Edward Louis Spiers, third from left. On Churchill's left is General Fayolle, commander of the 33rd Corps
Despite his having once been a professional soldier, Churchill's experience had no relevance to the grimness of trench warfare. He spent a month with the Grenadier Guards undergoing training. After visiting the French front line in December 1915 with his friend Captain Spiers (later Spears), he wrote to Clementine: 'I lunched with the HQ of the 33rd Corps and cheered them all up about the war & the future. The general insisted on our being photographed together [with] me in my French steel helmet & to make a background German prisoners were lined up...'

Churchill admired his friend Spiers' intelligence and bravery and would have been aware of his insight while acting as the liaison officer between the French and the British. On 23 August 1914, Spiers informed Sir John French of General Lanrezac's sudden decision to retreat – exposing the British forces on his flank. Spiers amazed himself by urging Lanrezac to launch a counter attack, adding, 'Mon Général, if by action the British Army is annihilated, England will never pardon France, and France will not be able to afford to pardon you.'

During the Gallipoli campaign (25 April 1915 – 9 January 1916), occasional truces were called to bury the dead
While Churchill was in France, the Gallipoli campaign continued to its bitter end. Jimmy Page, a British soldier who served in the Dardanelles, described the campaign as 'a very good idea, but a king-sized cock-up. And a lot of lives wasted in a useless endeavour.' Ordinary Seaman Joe Murray, Hood Battalion, Royal Naval Division, remembered 'Colonel

Quilter saying on the boat, just before we landed, that the eyes of the world would be upon us. Well, the eyes of the Turks certainly were, and so were their rifles, but the rest of the world seemed to have forgotten us.'

On 15 November 1915, Churchill wrote: '[I]t seems to me that if there were any operations in the history of the world which, having been begun, it was worth while to carry through with the utmost vigour and fury, with a consistent flow of reinforcements, and an utter disregard of life, it was the operation so daringly and brilliantly begun by Sir Ian Hamilton in the immortal landing of the 25th April.' However, after more than eight months of incompetence, disease and death, on 29 December the Allies began the evacuation of Gallipoli. On the Western Front, Douglas Haig replaced Sir John French as commander of the BEF.

'I have been given a fine steel helmet by the French,'
Churchill wrote to Clementine on 8 December 1915,
'wh[ich] I am going to wear, as it looks so nice & will
perhaps protect my valuable cranium.'

<u>Left:</u> *Winston Churchill Wearing a French Poilu's Steel Helmet*, Sir John Lavery (1856–1941), oil on canvas, 1916
According to Sir John Lavery, it was after Winston left the Admiralty and had more leisure time that the artist and his wife taught him to paint seriously in oils. Lavery also painted Churchill in his uniform, wearing his striking headgear, the steel helmet of a *poilu* – a French infantryman. This painting was commissioned by the officers of the Armoured Car Squadrons, in gratitude for Churchill's encouragement of them.

<u>Below:</u> Churchill with the officers of the 6th Royal Scots Fusiliers, Ploegsteert, Belgium, March 1916. On Churchill's right is his second-in-command, Sir Archibald Sinclair, later leader of the Liberal Party and Secretary of State for Air
In January 1916 Churchill took command of the 6th Battalion of the Royal Scots Fusiliers. Major Jock MacDavid described his arrival: 'Out of the first car came this well-known figure dressed in a long, fine-textured waterproof. He was wearing a *poilu* helmet and a Sam Browne belt holster with a revolver stuck well into it... I could hardly believe my eyes when I saw the second car, which was piled high with luggage... on the very top of all this clutter was a full-length tin bath. He gave a warm handshake, and introduced himself as Lieutenant Colonel Winston Churchill.'

Churchill opens a fête in aid of the Russian wounded and Scottish prisoners of war, Chelmsford, 9 September 1916

Having left his battalion in May 1916, Churchill resumed his seat in Parliament but was not offered a place in government. 'Is it not damnable that I should be denied all real scope to serve this country, in this tremendous hour?' he wrote to his brother on 15 July.

'What else is there in the world but the war? And what else is there in any of our minds but the war – the whole war and nothing but the war?' Churchill said in Chelmsford on 9 September. He continued, 'The great strength which our country has shown is a source of pride to everyone. The unanimity with which our Empire has rallied to the Mother Land in the great cause justifies and vindicates British institutions. It is over two years since the war began, and I well remember feeling at that time profoundly convinced that in declaring war on Germany our country had performed the most noble deed in all its history. We have gone through a lot since then: terrible losses, many disasters, bitter disappointments, but I never felt more sure... that the course we took two years ago was absolutely right – and that our children will live to bless the day and to glorify the deed.'

Churchill visits a munitions factory at Ponders End, north London, July 1917. Artillery shells are on display, as is the American flag – a tribute to Britain's new ally

On 7 December 1916, Lloyd George replaced Asquith as Prime Minister. Amid Conservative opposition, Lloyd George appointed Churchill Minister for Munitions in July 1917. Having experienced the effects of artillery at the Front, Churchill took an informed interest in the munitions industry, and was able to assure workers of their vital importance to the war effort.

In the following months he made several visits to France, where a château not far from the front line served as his headquarters. In September 1917, Eddie Marsh, who travelled with him on one of these visits, wrote: 'Winston was attracted by the sight of shells bursting in the distance – irresistible! Out we got, put on our steel helmets, hung our gas-masks round our necks, and walked for half-an-hour towards the firing, there was a great noise, shells whistling over our heads, and some fine bursts in the distance – but we seemed to get no nearer, and the firing died down, so we went back after another hour's delay... Winston's disregard of time, when there's anything he wants to do, is sublime – he firmly believes that it waits for him.'

Churchill's previous war experience –of horses charging into battle –had now almost become redundant. For more than a year he was to oversee the production of guns, tanks, aeroplanes and munitions.

Churchill surrounded by admirers at Beardmore's Gun Works, Glasgow, 8 October 1918

On 8 October 1918 Churchill visited Glasgow and, at a public meeting held there, he firmly stated that any defeatism or over-optimism about the war 'should be stamped out... with all the vigour of public opinion'.

'It might be that the course of the battle will be better than we have any right to hope for now,' he continued, 'but we must not count or build upon too favourable a development of events. We have started out to put this business through, and we must continue to develop to the utmost every resource that we can make certain that, whatever the course of the war in 1918, the year 1919 will see our foe unable to resist our legitimate and rightful claims.'

'I am so glad that it has all come right,' Churchill telegraphed to Haig at the end of the war. Haig replied, 'I shall always remember with gratitude the energy and foresight which you displayed as Minister of Munitions, and so rendered our success possible.'

Churchill watches the 47th Division march through the Grande Place, Lille, 29 October 1918

Churchill is seen here on the saluting stand in Lille, watching a march-past of British troops who had liberated the French city 11 days earlier. Though none of those in this picture would have known when the end was coming, they were in no doubt that, after years of stalemate, the Allies were now at last making rapid advances. 'It is rather an awful spectacle,' Clementine wrote to Winston on 29 October 1918, 'two great Empires cracking, swaying & on the verge of toppling into ruins.'

Behind the rather reflective Churchill stands Eddie Marsh, wearing a bowler hat, and directly above him, looking upward, is Churchill's brother Jack. The officer standing in front of Winston is Major Bernard Montgomery, whom he did not yet know.

Eddie Marsh remained Churchill's friend and adviser, following him from office to office throughout the many vicissitudes of his career. He was to write later: 'It was an understood thing, that I was Ruth to his Naomi, and that whither he went, so long as it was not into the actual Wilderness, where I should have no visible means of support, I should go.'

Only two days after the event pictured here, Turkey surrendered, soon to be followed by Austria-Hungary and then Germany on 11 November 1918.

5

Rising
Through
The Ranks:
1919–1928

The Prince of Wales had been keen to participate in the First World War. He joined the Grenadier Guards in August 1914, but Lord Kitchener forbade him from fighting at the Front for fear of his being captured.

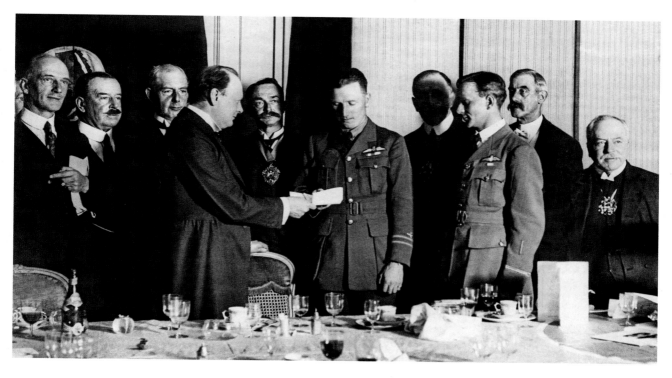

Opposite: Churchill, then Minister for War and Air, and Edward, Prince of Wales, at the House of Commons, 5 June 1919

Churchill and the Prince attended a luncheon in honour of three American airmen who had attempted to fly across the Atlantic. They could not be credited with the first non-stop crossing as their seaplane had had to alight on the water near the Azores due to thick fog before continuing to Lisbon.

When Churchill met the Prince of Wales (later King Edward VIII) at Balmoral six years earlier, he had written to Clementine: 'He is so nice, & we have made rather friends. They are worried a little about him, as he has become very Spartan – rising at 6 & eating hardly anything. He requires to fall in love with a pretty cat who will prevent him from getting too strenuous.' It was unfortunate for Churchill that the cat turned out to be Mrs Wallis Simpson. Winston supported Edward throughout this relationship and the 1936 Abdication Crisis, much to Clementine's displeasure.

Above: Churchill presents a cheque to the aviators Alcock and Brown at the House of Lords, 21 June 1919

On 14–15 June 1919, British aviators John Alcock and Arthur Whitten Brown flew non-stop across the Atlantic in a Vickers Vimy aeroplane. In recognition of their achievement, they were presented with a cheque for £10,000 from the *Daily Mail*. Probably inspired by their courageous flight, Churchill resumed flying lessons a month later, despite his pledge to Clementine. He crashed at Croydon Aerodrome. 'I feel dreadfully for Clemmy,' his cousin Lady Londonderry wrote. 'I really think it rather evil of you – but I do hope you have not been hurt.' Churchill again agreed to give up flying.

In his official capacity, Churchill was responsible for, and a great advocate of, the RAF, newly formed from the Royal Flying Corps and the Royal Naval Air Service in April 1918, and was instrumental in the establishment of the RAF's Officer Training College at Cranwell.

Of Churchill's appointment as Secretary of State for War and Air in February 1919, Clementine said: '[it is] like keeping a lot of balls in the air at the same time. After all, you want to be a Statesman, not a juggler.'

Above: **Churchill inspects the British Army of Occupation in Cologne, 16 August 1919. Field Marshal Sir Henry Wilson (Chief of the Imperial General Staff) is to Churchill's left, with Sir Archibald Sinclair (now Churchill's military secretary), between them**

On the second day of his visit to the British Army of Occupation in Cologne in August 1919, Churchill was to learn that the anti-Bolshevik forces were advancing in Russia. He returned to London to explain the situation to Lloyd George, who told him to let the Russians fight out their own quarrels at their own expense.

Despite Churchill's enthusiasm for flying, Clementine had suggested that he 'give up the Air & continue concentrating on what you are doing at the War Office... It would be a sign of real strength to do so, & people would admire it very much. It is weak to hang on to two offices – you really are only doing the one. Or again, if you swallow the two you will have violent indigestion.'

Opposite: **Churchill and Field Marshal Haig welcome General Armando Diaz, Chief of Staff of the Italian Army, at Victoria Station, London, 24 October 1919**

After Haig's death in 1928, Churchill wrote: 'Napoleon and the great Captains before him rode on the field amid their troops in the ardour of battle, and amid the perils of the storm. How gladly would Haig have welcomed the chance to mount his horse as he had done when a mere Corps Commander in the First Ypres, and ride slowly forward among the exploding shells! But all this is supposed to be forbidden to the modern Commander-in-Chief. He is lucky if even an aeroplane bomb, or some long-range projectile near Headquarters, relieves at rare intervals by its physical reminder the inward stress of mind. No anodyne of danger, no relief in violent action; nothing but anxiety, suspense, perplexing and contradictory information; weighing the imponderable, assigning proportions to what cannot be measured, intricate staff duties, difficult personal negotiations, and the mutterings of far-distant guns.

'But he endured it all; and with such impassivity and matter-of-fact day-to-day routine that I ... doubted whether he was not insensitive and indurated to the torment and drama in the shadow of which he dwelt. But when I saw after the War was over, for the first time, the historic "Backs to the Wall" document written before sunrise on that fateful April morning in 1918, and that it was no product of some able staff officer in the bureau,

but written with his own precise hand, pouring out without a check or correction the pent-up passion of his heart, my vision of the man assumed a new scale and colour. The Furies indeed contended in his soul; and that arena was large enough to contain their strife.'

<u>Right:</u> **Winston and his son Randolph, c. September 1920**
Randolph Churchill was a pupil at Sandroyd Prep in Cobham, Surrey, from 1920 until 1924, before going on to enrol at his grandfather Randolph's old school, Eton.

Clementine wrote to Winston on 31 March 1920: 'This week has been occupied in taking Randolph to have his school clothes fitted. He looks such a thin shrimp in trousers and an Eton collar!'

Winston wrote to Clementine on 14 February 1921: 'I went to see Randolph yesterday at Sandroyd and found him very well and very sprightly. The Headmaster described him as very combative, and said that on any pretext or excuse he mixes himself up in fights and quarrels; but they seemed pleased with him all the same.'

The 2nd Earl of Birkenhead, Churchill's godson and the son of F. E. Smith, described Winston's early relationship with his son thus: 'He over-compensated in his relationship with Randolph, making light of his bad reports, spoiling him and encouraging impertinence and independence which were already extraordinary in a child of his age.'

Winston and Clementine Churchill, T. E. Lawrence and Gertrude Bell, Cairo, 20 March 1921

On 15 February 1921, Churchill became Secretary of State for the Colonies and appointed Colonel T. E. Lawrence ('Lawrence of Arabia') as his Arab Affairs Advisor.

Three weeks later, he went to Cairo where, in conference with his Middle East advisers, he set up two Arab kingdoms (in Transjordan and Iraq) and confirmed Britain's promise to the Jews of a 'National Home' in Palestine. On a break from the conference,

Churchill, Clementine and his two leading advisors, Gertrude Bell (nicknamed 'Queen of the Desert') and Lawrence, visited the Pyramids on camels. The only woman among about 40 delegates, Bell had been invited to draw up the boundaries of Mesopotamia.

Lawrence died after a motorcycle accident in May 1935. Churchill wrote of him: 'His grip upon the imagination of the modern world was due to his indifference to all the delights which nature offers to her multitudes of children. He could feel her pangs to

the full. Her prizes did not stir him. Home, money, comfort, fame, power itself – meant little or nothing to him. The modern world had no means of exerting the slightest pull upon him. Solitary, austere, inexorable, he moved upon a plane apart from and above our common lot... I deem him one of the greatest beings alive in our time... we shall never see his like again.' King George V wrote of Lawrence: 'His name will live in history... It will live in the annals of war... It will live in the legends of Arabia.'

From Cairo, Churchill went to Jerusalem, where he told Emir Abdullah – later the first ruler of the new kingdom in Transjordan – that Palestine was to remain a British Mandate and open to Jewish settlers.

Churchill with T. E. Lawrence and the Emir Abdullah, the Palestine Mandate, 28 March 1921
On 14 June, after Churchill's return to England, he told the House of Commons: 'I was driven into a fertile and thriving country estate, where the scanty soil gave way to good crops and good cultivation, and then to vineyards and finally to the most beautiful, luxurious orange groves, all created in 20 or 30 years by the exertions of the Jewish community who live there... I defy anybody, after seeing work of this kind, achieved by so much labour, effort and skill, to say that the British government, having taken up the position it has, could cast it all aside and leave it to be rudely and brutally overturned by the incursion of a fanatical attack by the Arab population from outside.'

'The hope of your race for so many centuries will be gradually realized here,' Churchill said at the tree-planting ceremony in Jerusalem, 'not only for your own good but for the good of all the world.'

Churchill with Sir Herbert Samuel, British High Commissioner in Palestine, at a tree-planting ceremony, Mount Scopus, Jerusalem, March 1921
In March 1921, Churchill planted a tree on Mount Scopus at the site of the future Hebrew University in northeastern Jerusalem. He was accompanied by Sir Herbert Samuel, who later became the first Jewish leader of the Liberal Party, a position he held from 1931 to 1935.

At the ceremony, Churchill stated that the non-Jewish inhabitants must not suffer: 'Every step you take should therefore be also for moral and material benefit of all Palestinians.' Churchill went on to say: 'If you do this, Palestine will be happy and prosperous, and peace and concord will always reign; it will turn into a paradise...in which sufferers of all races and religions will find a rest from their sufferings.'

Churchill and Lloyd George at the Cenotaph, London, November 1921

The Cenotaph, designed by Edwin Lutyens and built from Portland stone, was unveiled in Whitehall on 11 November 1920. It is inscribed to 'The Glorious Dead'. Prior to the unveiling, the coffin of the Unknown Warrior was brought from Flanders to the Cenotaph, before being taken to be buried at Westminster Abbey.

While Churchill was away in Cairo, changes were made to the Cabinet and his hoped-for position of Chancellor of the Exchequer was taken up by Sir Robert Horne. He remained very displeased with Lloyd George for some time: on 26 April 1921, the Prime Minister's secretary wrote in her diary that 'Winston is still very vexed … as a result of having been neglected in the recent promotions.' Aware of this situation, Clementine urged her husband not to seek quarrels with Lloyd George: 'I do feel that as long as he is PM it would be better to hunt with him than to lie in the bushes & watch him careering along with jaundiced eye.'

Aside from mourning the men who died in Flanders, in 1921 the Churchills also had their own grief to bear, after Clementine's brother Bill committed suicide in April, followed in June by the death of Winston's mother, Jennie. And worst of all, in August, their daughter Marigold died of septicaemia of the throat, at the age of two and a half. Churchill had been devoted to 'the Duckadilly' and was crushed by her death.

Churchill arrives at the Savoy for lunch with Lloyd George, London, 2 March 1922

By 1922, Churchill found himself increasingly out of sympathy with the Liberals. His friendship with Lloyd George continued on a personal level, but they had serious professional disagreements. The problems with Russia caused rifts between them, leading Lloyd George to say that Churchill's obsession with the issue had reached the level of fanaticism. The Prime Minister considered that a war-weary public would not support yet more fighting, and in fact there was considerable sympathy among the British working-class for the Bolshevist cause. However his Coalition government soon collapsed.

In October that year, Churchill almost died from acute appendicitis. On 15 November, the Conservatives won the general election and Churchill lost his constituency of Dundee. Later he commented: 'In the twinkling of an eye, I found myself without an office, without a seat, without a party and without an appendix.'

Churchill stands as the candidate for West Leicester in the general election, December 1923

In November 1923, Prime Minister Stanley Baldwin announced that he was calling a general election. Seven Liberal associations wanted Churchill to be their candidate. He accepted the invitation of West Leicester.

When Churchill spoke in the constituency during the electoral campaign, someone in the crowd shouted the familiar question, 'What about the Dardanelles?' He responded: '[P]eople who in the war filled positions of awful responsibility and had to take terrible decisions have the right to be judged leniently and generously by their fellow-countrymen. I believe history will show they acted for the best, and will record its opinion that this was the right thing to do, and that if one could have got more power and influence to push it through with vigour it would have made an enormous difference and would have saved us the torments and tortures of the last two years of the war. Don't imagine I am running away from the Dardanelles. I glory in it.'

The election was held on 6 December 1923. Churchill lost.

Winston and Clementine with Mary (aged two) at Chartwell, 1924

On 15 September 1922, Clementine gave birth to her fifth child, a daughter who was christened Mary. Also on that day Churchill bought Chartwell for £5,000, scarcely more than the annual income from an inheritance he derived from a distant cousin: Lord Henry Vane-Tempest had been killed in a railway accident in 1921 and left him £4,000 a year. For the next 40 years, Chartwell became Winston's home – a place to work, relax, swim, paint, write and, most importantly, to be with his wife and family. However, Mary Churchill later said that for Clementine, 'Chartwell was never to be...the place of pleasure, fun, and unalloyed happiness it was from the beginning for Winston.'

Winston and Mary at Chartwell, 1924

On 15 March 1925, Churchill wrote to Clementine that 'Mary is flourishing. She comes & sits with me in the mornings & is sometimes most gracious.'

Churchill and his secretary Lettice Fisher at his home in Sussex Square, London, 6 March 1924

Throughout 1923 and 1924, Churchill tried to return to Parliament. After the defeat at West Leicester for the Liberal Party, he next stood in a by-election for the Abbey Division of Westminster, as an Independent Constitutionalist.

Starting on 5 March 1924, Churchill worked hard with his secretary Lettice Fisher on his by-election campaign. The next day, his candidature became the focus of national attention and interest, and *The Times* denounced him as 'an essentially disruptive force'.

'He is being rung up at his house,' the *Evening News* reported, 'as few people ever have been in the history of the telephone.' Clementine hurried back from the south of France to help him.

Fisher was very much needed at this time, but for the next few years there is little mention of her, although she presumably was still useful to Churchill. In 1928, she helped him type up Volume IV of *The World Crisis*, as he comments in a letter to Clemmie (probably also typewritten by Fisher): 'I have been working fairly hard, and so has Miss Fisher...nearly 3, 000 words in the last two days!'

With support from significant sections of the London press, who backed him as a personality rather than in support of a Unionist/Liberal coalition, Churchill came very close to winning the Abbey by-election.

Left: **Churchill shakes hands with supporters at the Abbey by-election, 20 March 1924**

Churchill's main rival was the Conservative candidate, Otto Nicholson. Winston's relationship with the Conservatives was fraught. 'Do not however let the Tories get you too cheap,' Clementine wrote to her husband on 24 February 1924. 'They have treated you so badly in the past & they ought to be made to feel it... my Darling do not stand unless you are reasonably sure of getting in – The movement inside the Tory Party to try & get you back is only just born & requires nursing & nourishing & educating to bring it to full strength.'

Churchill wrote to Clementine on the same day that 'it is an amazing constituency comprising – Eccleston Sq., Victoria Station, Smith Sq., Westminster Abbey, Whitehall, Pall Mall, Carlton House Terrace – part of Soho, the south side of Oxford Street, Drury Lane theatre & Covent Garden! It is of course one of the choicest preserves of the Tory Party.'

Above: **Churchill addresses his supporters after his defeat at Abbey**

After the announcement of his loss to Nicholson by 43 votes and the confirmation that the Abbey seat would remain Conservative, Churchill rallied: 'I do not believe that the Conservative Party can afford to reject and repulse the forces which are represented in the 8,000 votes for an Independent Anti-Socialist candidate. I do not believe that narrow, bitter party views or weak, incoherent party action will receive the approval of the mass of patriotic, loyal, progressive British men and women throughout the land, who see very clearly the direction in which the leaders of the historic parties ought to lead their followers. I am content to let this lesson be studied in all parts of the country, and I predict that the course of events in the next few months, and certainly within a year, will show very clearly the foresight, the clarity of judgment, the patriotic resolution, which has animated all those who have fought this contest on my side.'

In his manifesto for the safe Tory seat of Epping, Churchill declared, 'I give my whole support to the Conservative Party', and went on to say that there was 'no gulf of principle' between Tories and Liberals.

Below: **Churchill and Clementine enjoy Winston's election success on a tour of Epping, 21 October 1924. Holding the reins of the coach is Claud F. Goddard, one of his supporters**

Due to the fall of the Labour government, another general election was held in October 1924 – the third in three years. The Conservatives won convincingly and Churchill, supported by them, finally returned to Parliament, winning the seat at Epping by a majority of 9,763 votes. He was to remain the MP for Epping (later renamed the Wanstead and Woodford Division of Essex) for the last 40 years of his political life. In 1925 he rejoined the Conservative Party, which he had left 21 years previously.

Above: **Churchill addresses his new constituency, Epping, 21 October 1924**

On 11 September 1924, Churchill accepted the nomination for a safe Conservative seat, Epping, although he officially ran as a 'Constitutionalist'. In his manifesto, he declared Socialism to be the enemy, and that Labour was failing at fighting it.

In his election address on 12 October, he attacked the Labour leader Ramsay MacDonald : 'Spellbound by the lure of Moscow, wire-pulled through subterranean channels... MacDonald and his associates have attempted to make the British nation accomplices in Bolshevist crimes.'

Churchill playing polo, 1924

Churchill played polo for three decades, having become a devotee of the sport when he was posted to Bangalore. This was all the more impressive as he had dislocated his right shoulder in India in 1896, rendering him unable to lift a polo mallet above the shoulder. He continued to play until he was 51, with his right arm strapped to his chest.

Even after he had given up playing polo, Winston continued to ride for pleasure until he was in his eighties.

He was passionate about horses and riding: 'And here I say to parents, especially wealthy parents, "Don't give your son money. As far as you can afford it, give him horses." No one ever came to grief – except honourable grief – through riding horses. No hour of life is lost that is spent in the saddle. Young men have often been ruined through owning horses, or through backing horses, but never through riding them; unless of course they break their necks, which taken at a gallop is a very good death to die.'

As a member of the Conservative government, Churchill continued to show his independence of mind. 'He is a Chimborazo or Everest among the sand-hills of the Baldwin Cabinet,' declared Asquith.

Churchill with Prime Minister Baldwin (centre) and Foreign Secretary Austen Chamberlain in Downing Street, after the Allied Financial Conference in Paris, January 1925
After the election of 1924, Churchill became Chancellor of the Exchequer in Stanley Baldwin's Conservative government. On 6 January 1925 he went to Paris for the Allied Financial Conference where, after a week of intense negotiations, he secured a memorable settlement of the international war debts: Britain would now pay her £1,000 million debt, which the United States had been demanding, in instalments while at the same time receiving payments from France, Belgium, Italy and Japan.

On 8 January he said in Paris: 'Hope flies on wings, and Inter-Allied Conferences plod along dusty roads, but still the conviction exists that progress is being made towards the recognition of the unity and prosperity of Europe.'

All the parties involved admired Churchill's skill, patience and grasp of detail. Edward Grey, who had been Foreign Secretary at the outbreak of the war and had delivered the immortal lines, 'The lamps are going out all over Europe; we shall not see them lit again in our life-time', wrote to Churchill after the conference: 'To uphold the interests, & at the same time to secure this recognition from the representatives of other countries is a rare achievement & a great public service.'

Churchill with Sir Philip Cunliffe-Lister and Detective-Sergeant Walter Thompson (in the back seat), 1925

Sir Philip Cunliffe-Lister (later the Earl of Swinton) was a friend of Churchill who became as a cabinet minister in the 1930s. Together they did their utmost to promote the re-arming of Britain, despite government opposition.

In 1920, when Churchill became a target during the particularly violent Irish Troubles, Walter Thompson of the Special Branch had been detailed to guard him, which he did until the early 1930s. At the outbreak of war in 1939 Thompson was recalled from retirement and once more became Churchill's personal bodyguard, remaining with him until 1945. Thompson went wherever Churchill did and they naturally became close through the years: Thompson observed that 'during the war years I spent more time with him than any other human'. Churchill wrote to Clementine from Chartwell: 'Thompson and I have been wallowing in the filthiest black mud you ever saw, with the vilest odour.' She did not feel the same way as Winston did about the bodyguard, and Thompson could tell – he wrote later in his memoirs: 'I was a perpetual annoyance to her.'

**Churchill at the Woodford Girls'
School's summer fête in his Epping
constituency, summer 1925**

On 28 April 1925, Churchill made his
first Budget speech, announcing the
government's intention to return to
the international gold standard at its
pre-war parity. However, this return
– at an exchange rate of £1 to $4.66
– proved to be far too high, with the
result that the British economy found
itself in the grips of a deflation that
lasted until the country was forced
off gold in 1931.

Despite this and many other
problems, Churchill found time to
attend the summer fête at a school
in his constituency of Epping. This
visit, and with the Great War still at
the back of his mind as well as time
he had spent recently in war-torn
France, made him think about the
consequences of another war: 'Is this
the end? Is it to be merely a chapter in
a cruel and senseless story? Will a new
generation in their turn be immolated
to square the black accounts of Teuton
and Gaul? Will our children bleed
and gasp again in devastated lands?
Or will there spring from the very
fires of conflict that reconciliation of
the three giant combatants, which
would unite their genius and secure to
each in safety and freedom a share in
rebuilding the glory of Europe?'

'The Irish Question can only be settled when the human question is settled,' Churchill told Parliament in December 1925.

Above: **Churchill on his way to the Ulster Hall in Belfast, 3 March 1926**
Having been presented with a 'paddy' hat and a shillelagh, Churchill was driven around Belfast in an Irish 'jaunting car' while visiting the city in March 1926, during Queen's University's Rag Week. This was certainly a change from his visits to the city earlier in the decade. Churchill had been deeply involved with the Irish Troubles. He worked with Sir Henry Wilson, security advisor to the Irish goverment, and Michael Collins, the leading Irish negotiator of the Irish Treaty; by 1922 both men had been murdered for their involvement in the talks. Shortly before his death, Collins sent a message to London: 'Tell Winston we could never have done anything without him.' The police believed that Churchill might also become a victim of a murder plot, so he travelled in an armoured car and was always accompanied by Walter Thompson.

Opposite: **Winston and Clementine Churchill with their children Randolph and Diana, 1926**
On 4 May 1926, the Trades Union Congress called a general strike. Transport, printing and building workers, among others, walked out in support of the miners, who were facing a cut in wages. During the strike, Churchill organized the printing of the *British Gazette* and determined a policy of 'no surrender' to the strikers. 'The nation remains calm and confident,' he declared, 'and the people are bearing with fortitude and good temper the inestimable hardships of a national crisis.' The strike ended on 19 May, although the miners themselves did not return to work until five months later. After praising the courage of the Prime Minister and others, the *Daily Mail* wrote: 'Nor can the services of Winston Churchill be overlooked. His energy and initiative have never been more clearly shown in a great cause.'

With the strike over, Churchill endeavoured to persuade the mine owners to make concessions to the miners, but they refused. Churchill warned that 'either the country will break the General Strike, or the General Strike will break the country'.

Churchill wrote to Clementine of their daughter Diana, who was 16: '[She] is going to be a gt feature in our lives in the next few years. Nature is mysteriously arming her for the ancient conflict. She has a wonderful charm & grace, wh grows now perceptibly from month to month.'

Churchill, accompanied by his daughter Diana and his bodyguard Walter Thompson, walks to the Houses of Parliament on Budget Day, 11 April 1927
MPs crowded into the House, as was usual, to hear Churchill's third Budget speech. Prime Minister Stanley Baldwin described the scene to the King: '[It was] was quite sufficient to show that Mr Churchill as a star turn has a power of attraction which nobody in the House of Commons can excel.' He went on to describe Churchill's 'undercurrent of buoyant mischievousness which frequently makes its appearance on the surface in some picturesque phrase or playful sally at the expense of his opponents'. Of the subject of Churchill's Budget itself, Baldwin said: 'His enemies will say that this year's Budget is a mischievous piece of manipulation and juggling with the country's finances, but his friends will say that it is a masterpiece of ingenuity.'

In this photograph, Walter Thompson, walking on Churchill's right, is seen with his hand on his revolver in his coat pocket, ready in case of an attempt on Churchill's life.

Churchill strides confidently from the sea at Deauville, France, August 1927

In 1906 Churchill had left England for a lengthy holiday at Deauville and between the two World Wars he and Clementine also went frequently to France, staying with English friends who had houses there.

In the summer of 1927, Clementine was knocked down by a bus on the Brompton Road in London, and the accident left her badly shaken. Although concerned about his wife, Churchill continued to work on the third volume of *The World Crisis*, his history of the First World War, first at Chartwell and later in Scotland as well as in France, before joining her in Venice, where she had been sent to recuperate for six weeks.

The book was published later that year, and it was evident that the horror of the Great War was still with Churchill. He reflected on France that 'only the cemeteries, the monuments and stunted steeples with here and there a mouldering trench or huge mine-crater lake, assail the traveller with the fact that twenty-five millions of soldiers fought here and twelve millions shed their blood or perished in the greatest of all human contentions less than ten years ago'.

According to Winston's daughter Mary,
the Churchill family Christmas at Chartwell
'was always a glorious feast'.

Churchill applies the finishing touches to his snowman at Chartwell, Christmas 1927

On Christmas Eve 1927, southern England was hit with heavy snowfalls. Some villages in Kent were completely cut off by the blizzard and supplies had to be airlifted in, but the Churchills did not seem to encounter major problems at Chartwell.

Winston's daughter Mary described Christmases at Chartwell: 'The same party usually assembled: Winston and Clementine and their four children; Jack and Goonie [Winston's brother and sister-in-law], with Johnnie, Peregrine and Clarissa [their children]; Bertram and Nellie Romilly with Giles and Esmond [Clementine's sister, her husband and sons]. The only "outsiders" were Professor Lindemann [later Lord Cherwell] and sometimes Eddie Marsh.' The family also enjoyed 'amateur theatricals' at Chartwell, as 'the dining room made a splendid theatre'. The Great Snow of 1927 brought even more fun, especially for the older children who 'constructed a marvellous igloo; there was a snowman, tobogganing, and skating on the lake'.

For Churchill, Christmas offered a much-needed break from working furiously on a scheme to abolish the system of local rates and stop rising unemployment and falling trade. A few days before Christmas, he sent the first copy of this scheme to Baldwin, calling it 'My Best Endeavour'.

Randolph Churchill (aged 16), Coco Chanel and Winston Churchill, Dampierre, France, 8 April 1928
Winston and Clementine would often stay with the Duke of Westminster, who was one of Winston's greatest friends as well as an incomparable host, with houses in France, at Eaton Hall near Chester and in Scotland.

The Duke's marriage to his wife Violet had ended in divorce in 1926 and he began a relationship with Coco Chanel, the French fashion designer. In 1927 she joined a hunting party in the Forêt d'Eu in Normandy and Churchill described their meeting: 'The famous Coco turned up & I took a gt fancy to her – A most capable & agreeable woman – much the strongest personality Bennie [the Duke] has yet been up against. She hunted vigorously all day, motored to Paris after dinner, & is today engaged in passing & improving dresses on endless streams of mannequins. Altogether 200 models have to be settled in about 3 weeks. Some have to be altered ten times. She does it with her own fingers, pinning, cutting, looping etc...'

Churchill on a wild boar hunt in the Forêt d'Eu, Normandy, 31 January 1927
One of Churchill's favourite activities when visiting the Duke of Westminster in France was boar hunting. In January 1927, Clementine remained at home while her husband and Randolph made a tour of Europe. Winston wrote to her from Dieppe: 'Yesterday we hunted the penwiper [wild boar]. A dramatic moment occurred when he appeared from a lake where he had refreshed himself & galloped into our midst.' Clemmie, however, replied: '[M]ore exciting than the "penwiper" is your account of "Coco".'

Churchill working on the brick wall at Chartwell with his daughter Sarah, 3 September 1928

Churchill enjoyed participating in major building works at Chartwell, such as the construction of a dam, a swimming pool and a red-brick wall built to surround the large vegetable garden. On 2 September 1928, he wrote to Baldwin: 'I have had a delightful month, building a cottage and dictating a book: 200 bricks and 2,000 words a day.'

A photograph of Winston working on a brick wall at Chartwell, similar to the one shown here but without Sarah, was published in the *Daily Sketch* with the caption: 'Those who may be inclined to point out that he has not got his coat off should bear in mind that he took it off when he was helping to lay the foundations, and that, anyhow, he is wearing an old suit. He lays one brick a minute.'

The Mayor of Battersea invited Churchill to join the Amalgamated Union of Building Trades Workers. Churchill, having led the suppression of the General Strike two years before, appreciated the humour of the idea and consented to become a member. However the union, less than impressed, sent his money back.

Churchill continued this pastime for years to come. 'Each afternoon, we'd spend a couple of hours together, laying bricks,' his grandson Winston recalled. 'If anyone had asked me what my grandfather did, I'd have said: "He's a bricklayer."'

6

The Wilderness Years: 1929–1939

On 15 April 1929 Churchill delivered his fifth and final Budget, the first Chancellor of the Exchequer to achieve this feat since William Gladstone.

Churchill flanked by his son Randolph and Lord Derby, Lord Lieutenant of Lancashire, general election rally, Liverpool, May 1929

The campaign for the general election of May 1929 was undramatic. The Conservatives' slogan of 'Safety First', which referred to the party's strict economic policy, did not capture the public's hearts. Churchill warned voters that a Labour government would 'bring back the Russian Bolsheviks, who will immediately get busy in the mines and factories, as well as among the armed forces, planning another General Strike'. However, he knew that memories of the previous strike cut deep and soon accepted that defeat was inevitable. The Conservatives lost to Labour, but there was no overall majority. This meant that Ramsay MacDonald's second government would need the support of the Liberals, led by Lloyd George. Churchill at least won his seat at Epping over the Liberal candidate.

The 1929 general election was memorable for being the first in which all women over the age of 21 were allowed to vote – previously it had been only women over 30 who also met specific property requirements.

Churchill's furniture is removed from 11 Downing Street, June 1929

The Conservative defeat was a blow to Churchill. Convinced that the only way to take on Labour was to form a Conservative-Liberal alliance, he met Lloyd George in June 1927 to discuss this possibility. In June, T. E. Lawrence wrote of Churchill to Eddie Marsh: 'He's a good fighter and will do better out than in, and will come back in a stronger position than before. I want him to be PM somehow.'

Nationalism was rising in Egypt and the dismissal of the High Commissioner, after MacDonald declared his decision to withdraw British troops from Cairo to the Suez Canal, angered Churchill. 'I reacted vehemently against this rough and sudden gesture,' he wrote later. 'But Mr Baldwin ... did not think that this was good ground for a fight with the Government. It would unite the Liberals with them and leave the Conservatives in a marked minority.'

Churchill also started writing the biography of his ancestor, the 1st Duke of Marlborough, and employed a young historian, Maurice Ashley, to travel to archives around the country to bring him back source material.

143

'What fun it is to get away from England,' Churchill wrote in 1929, 'and to feel one has no responsibility for her exceedingly tiresome and embarrassing affairs.'

Churchill with his son Randolph, nephew Johnnie and brother Jack, Calgary, Canada, August 1929
Free from governmental duties, Churchill embarked on a three-month holiday to Canada and the US, where he gave speeches and lectures. 'Randolph has conducted himself in a most dutiful manner and is an admirable companion,' Churchill wrote to Clementine from Ottawa on 15 August 1929. 'I think he has made a good impression on everybody.

He is taking a most intelligent interest in everything, and is a remarkable critic and appreciator of the speeches I make and the people we meet.' He went on: 'Today a former Sergeant of the Engineers, who helped me in '98...make my plans for the battle of Omdurman for *The River War*, held me up in the street, introduced himself and presented me with a box of excellent cigars for use on my journey. He was in quite humble circumstances and I was greatly touched...'

Churchill with his catch, a 188lb swordfish it took him 25 minutes to land, off Catalina Island, California, September 1929

On 29 September 1929, Churchill wrote to Clementine: '[W]e went on Sunday in a yacht to Catalina Island 25 miles away. We had only one hour there. People go for weeks & months without catching a swordfish – so they all said it was quite useless my going out in the fishing boat wh[ich] had been provided. However I went out & of course I caught a monster ...!'

Churchill returned to New York on 'Black Thursday', 24 October 1929, the day the New York stock market crashed. 'Under my window,' he wrote, 'a gentleman cast himself down fifteen storeys, and was dashed to pieces.'

He wrote of the Wall Street Crash: 'No one who gazed on such a scene could doubt that this financial disaster, huge as it is, cruel as it is to thousands, is only a passing episode in the march of a valiant and serviceable people who by fierce experiment are hewing new paths for man, and showing to all nations much that they should attempt and much that they should avoid.'

Churchill wrote of his love for cigars: 'How can I tell that my temper would have been as sweet or my companionship as agreeable if I had abjured from my youth the goddess Nicotine?'

Top right: **Churchill at the Banff Springs Hotel, Canadian Rockies, 6 September 1929**
Churchill's first order of cigars in 1900 consisted of 50 Bock Giraldas, and after that he thoroughly enjoyed smoking Cubanos. While in New York, he came across a cheaper alternative called Longfellows, his choice for the next ten years.

'How can I tell that the soothing influence of tobacco upon my nervous system may not have enabled me to comport myself with calm and with courtesy in some awkward personal encounter or negotiation, or carried me serenely through some critical hours of anxious waiting?' Churchill wrote. '[I]f I had not turned back to get that matchbox which I left behind in my dug-out in Flanders, might I not just have walked into the shell which pitched so harmlessly a hundred yards ahead?'

Opposite: **Churchill is appointed Chancellor of Bristol University, December 1929**
In 1925 Churchill had received an honorary degree from Bristol and in 1929 he was appointed Chancellor of the university, a position he held until his death. At the ceremony in Bristol, he was 'arrested' by students, who found him guilty 'of acquiring a new hat, a new chancellorship and with neglecting to supply forenoon coffee and biscuits to the students'.

'Arthur Balfour did not mingle in the hurly-burly. He glided upon its surface,' Churchill wrote. 'His aversion from the Roman Catholic faith was dour and inveterate. Otherwise he seemed to have the personal qualification of a great Pope.'

22nd February 1930

My dear Arthur,

It gave me so much pleasure to receive a letter from you and to know that you had been interested in the Russian début and débacle.

I have sent my much corrected proof of the "Marne" to the printer for you to have a clean copy. It should reach me Wednesday or Thursday and I will send the two next chapters on to you at once. I must tell you that both in the Tannenberg and the Marne episodes what I have written is solidly backed by our Official Military Historian, General Edmonds; and I do not think the general conclusions are likely to be disputed.

You will have been amused to see the Rothermere-Beaverbrook bid for power. They have greatly miscalculated the forces at work in our public life. They thought, and I daresay still think, that these two papers with their immense circulation would overturn the party hierarchy and leave them dictators of the political scene. As you once observed – and I have often agreed with it – "This is a singularly ill-contrived world, but not so ill-contrived as that". People always forget the reserve forces which come into play once a new level is reached or a new height attained.

Navy. I received a communication – quite informal – from the Foreign Office that a speech threatening the Government if they gave way any more would be extremely welcome to the present Prime Minister, so I am going to make one to the Navy League in the City on Wednesday next. I am going to give His Majesty's Government the support of a good hearty kick.

With every good wish,

The Rt. Hon. The Earl of Balfour,
            P.C., K.G., O.M.,
Fishers Hill,
Woking.

in the City on Wednesday next. I am going to give His Majesty's Government the support of a good hearty kick.

Letter from Churchill to Arthur Balfour, 22 February 1930

Less than a month after Churchill wrote him the letter shown here, Arthur Balfour died from phlebitis, which had incapacitated him since the previous year. On 22 March 1930, Churchill attended the memorial service for the former Prime Minister at Westminster Abbey.

A year later, he wrote of Balfour: 'When they took him to the Front to see the war, he admired with bland interest through his pince-nez the bursting shells. Luckily none came near enough to make him jump, as they will make any man jump, if they have their chance... [In December 1916] he passed from one Cabinet to the other, from the Prime Minister [Asquith] who was his champion, to the Prime Minister [Lloyd George] who had been his most powerful critic, like a powerful graceful cat walking delicately and unsoiled across a rather muddy street.'

Churchill and Brendan Bracken, 19 June 1930

Harold Macmillan likened Churchill's friendship with Brendan Bracken, the Conservative MP for North Paddington from 1929 to 1945, to the relationship of Aaron and Moses, with the younger man keeping Churchill's spirits high in the 'political wilderness'. They met in 1923, when Bracken contradicted Churchill at a lunch given by the *Observer* and their friendship lasted until Bracken's death in 1958. Vitally, Bracken helped Churchill, who had lost a considerable amount of money on the American stock market, with his financial affairs, negotiating an £8,000 deal for him with the *Daily Mail* for a series of articles and putting him in touch with Sir Henry Strakosch, a financier who helped him avoid bankruptcy.

Having seemingly arrived from nowhere, Bracken was soon of interest to many, with his striking appearance – bright red hair and pale skin – and his sudden great influence over Churchill. He was an inspiration for Evelyn Waugh's character Rex Mottram in *Brideshead Revisited*, while Stanley Baldwin called him Churchill's faithful *chela*, a Hindustani word for 'disciple'. Clementine was not particularly fond of Bracken, with his tendency to stay over uninvited and call her 'Clemmie', and matters were not helped by a rumour that suggested he could be Churchill's illegitimate son. When Clementine questioned her husband, he joked that he had checked but 'the dates don't coincide'.

In 1931, Baldwin supported Conservative participation in the proposed National Government. Lloyd George was opposed, but too unwell to prevent the new government, from which Churchill was excluded, from forming.

Above: **Churchill and Charlie Chaplin at Chartwell, summer 1931**

Churchill had become friends with Chaplin on his visit to Hollywood in 1929. He wrote to Clementine that 'you cd not help liking him...He is a marvellous comedian – bolshy in politics – delightful in conversation. He acted his new film for us... It is to be his gt attempt to prove that the silent drama or pantomime is superior to the new talkies...if pathos & wit will count for anything it ought to win an easy victory.'

In 1931, the actor attended a dinner at Chartwell. 'Chaplin opened the conversation by saying, "You made a great mistake when you went back to the gold standard at the wrong parity of exchange in 1925",' the MP Robert Boothby recalled. 'Churchill, who hated to be reminded of past mistakes, sank into a morose silence, a mood broken only when the comedian picked up two rolls of bread, put two forks in them and did the famous dance from [*The Gold Rush*].'

Right: **Churchill in Epping on election day, 27 October 1931**

In August 1931, MacDonald's Labour government crumbled. The King asked MacDonald to stay on as Prime Minister, but as the leader of a National Government made up of various parties. The general election held on 27 October saw an overwhelming response for this new government. The Conservatives won 473 seats, although committing to have MacDonald stay as Prime Minister. MacDonald's own Labour party won only 52 seats. Despite almost doubling his majority at Epping, Churchill was still given no governmental responsibility.

'I certainly suffered every pang, mental and physical, that a street accident or, I suppose, a shell wound can produce. None is unendurable,' Churchill told the *Daily Mail* after being hit by a car in New York.

Winston in a wheelchair while recovering from a car accident, New York, 21 December 1931

At the end of 1931, Churchill undertook another lecture tour of America. On 12 December, the day after his first lecture, he was knocked down by a car while crossing Fifth Avenue. He suffered severe shock and bruising, developed pleurisy and had to postpone his remaining lectures while he recuperated. Two weeks later he telegraphed the *Daily Mail*: 'There is neither the time nor the strength for self-pity. There is no room for remorse or fears. If at any moment in this long series of sensations a grey veil deepening into blackness had descended upon the sanctum I should have felt or feared nothing additional.'

Churchill leaves Beaumont Street Nursing Home, London, on a stretcher, 10 October 1932

While visiting the Duke of Marlborough's battlefields in Germany to conduct research for his biography, Churchill became ill with paratyphoid fever, which later led to a severe haemorrhage. On his return to Chartwell, his secretary Violet Pearman wrote: 'Mr Churchill is steadily improving, though progress is rather slow, but as usual nothing can keep him from work.' By the end of October, Churchill had finished half of the first of his Marlborough books.

Keep on hand ✓

O. C. PICKHARDT, M. D.
117 EAST 80TH STREET
NEW YORK

January 26, 1932.

This is to certify that the post-accident conva-
lescence of the Hon. Winston S. Churchill necessitates
the use of alcoholic spirits especially at meal times.
The quantity is naturally indefinite but the minimum
requirements would be 250 cubic centimeters.

Signed:-

OCP:P

OTTO C. PICKHARDT, M.D.

Churchill's prescription from Dr Otto C. Pickhardt, New York, 26 January 1932

Otto C. Pickhardt was a surgeon at New York's Lenox Hill Hospital, where he treated Churchill after his car accident. He also gave him this prescription for 'the use of alcoholic spirits especially at meal times' during his convalesence, despite America being in the grip of Prohibition.

The two men remained in contact, and when he was in England on duty during the Second World War, Pickhardt was invited to lunch with the Churchills at 10 Downing Street.

In 1916, on taking leave of the 6th Royal Scots Fusiliers, Churchill had stated: 'Whatever else they may say of me as a soldier, at least nobody can say I have ever failed to display a meet and proper appreciation of the virtues of alcohol.' In 1943 he was to comment wryly: 'I need a little more to drink. You see I have a war to fight and I need fortitude for the battle. And there is one favour I hope you will do for me. I hope that you will come to my defence if someday, someone should claim that I am a teetotaller.'

Opposite: **Churchill photographed by Edward Steichen, New York, 1932**
While on his speaking tour of America, Churchill posed for the celebrity photographer of the moment, Edward Steichen. The photograph was commissioned by *Vanity Fair* and the original magazine caption read, 'He has been a painter, author, soldier, polo player, bricklayer, foxhunter.'

A critic wrote about the renowned photographer that the 'worldly men of business and politics were invariably presented by Steichen in a setting as static as their own large offices. He could be confident that Churchill, for instance, would accept only the traditional seated-figure-against-a-dark-background format.'

Above: **Churchill at a Royal Academy banquet, London, 30 April 1932**
In 1932 Churchill made a speech at the Royal Academy in which he explained that he was not exhibiting his work there that year and also spoke of other politican-cum-artists, including Ramsay MacDonald, with his 'lurid sunsets of Empire and capitalist civilizations'. Of Stanley Baldwin, Churchill said: 'He is still quite a distinguished painter in our academy. If I were to criticize him at all I would say his work lacked a little in colour, and was also a little lacking in the precise definition of objects in the foreground.' In a letter to Churchill, Baldwin wrote that 'a kind word to the genre painter from so distinguished an exponent of a far different style shows a breadth of mind as rare as it is delightful'. To which Churchill replied: 'I was very glad that my chaff did not vex you. My shafts, though necessarily pointed, are never intentionally poisoned. If they cut, I pray they do not fester in the wound.'

Later, Churchill did submit works to the Academy's exhibition. His bodyguard Sergeant Murray was a fellow painter, but his artwork was rejected. Churchill told him: 'You know, your paintings are so much better than mine, but yours are judged on their merit.' So that his would be too, Churchill adopted a pseudonym. Two of his paintings were accepted and after his real identity was revealed, the title of Honorary Academician Extraordinary was bestowed upon him.

At heart, Churchill was a traditional man, joking that man's 'trusty friend the horse' had been replaced by the 'infernal combustion engine', but he sought to obtain some understanding of scientific advances, realizing their importance, especially in regards to war.

Left : Churchill escorts his daughter Diana to her wedding to John Bailey, London, 12 December 1932
John Milner Bailey, the son of the South African tycoon Sir Abe Bailey, married Diana Churchill at St Margaret's, Westminster, the church where her parents had wed. Sarah was a bridesmaid. Among the guests was Lloyd George.

The marriage was unhappy and by 1935 the couple had divorced. The same year, Diana married Duncan Sandys, who became the Conservative member for Norwood. They had met at a by-election where Randolph was campaigning against Sandys. They had three children – Julian, Edwina and Celia. In the 1950s, Diana suffered a severe nervous breakdown. She and Sandys divorced in 1960 and, three years later, Diana committed suicide.

Right : Churchill with Albert Einstein in the rose gardens at Chartwell, 1933
Two of the most influential minds of the twentieth century met in 1933. Churchill and Einstein discussed the scientific world and the growing threat of Germany. The creator of the world's most famous equation also turned his thoughts to politics: 'The situation in Europe has changed sharply within the past year; we should be playing into the hands of our bitterest enemies were we to close our eyes to this fact.' To an American professor, Einstein said: 'To prevent the greater evil, it is necessary that the lesser evil – the hated military – be accepted for the time being.'

Left: **Winston and Clementine board a plane from Croydon to Paris, September 1934**

On 25 September 1934, Churchill left Chartwell for a Mediterranean cruise aboard Lord Moyne's yacht *Rosaura*. After reaching Beirut, he and Clementine travelled overland through Lebanon, Syria, Palestine and Transjordan, visiting the ruins of Petra, where they spent the night. They then flew across the Sinai Desert to Cairo, where Churchill spent two happy days painting at the Pyramids before returning by yacht from Alexandria to Naples, and from there by train to Paris. The final lap of the journey was again by air, from Paris to Croydon, a short drive to Chartwell.

In December Clementine rejoined the *Rosaura* on her own, leaving behind a reluctant Winston, who did not want to be cooped up in a boat, removed from the political scene, for the duration of a lengthy voyage; he was also deeply engrossed in his work on the life of Marlborough. Although he viewed any separation from Clementine with considerable concern, he recognized that, in their life together, Clementine's preferences and plans had nearly always been subordinated to his own.

Right: **Churchill and a newspaper vendor, Middle East, October 1934**

In 1934, Churchill was winning an ever-widening public for the views he expressed in the press. A reader wrote to him: 'Your detachment from politics recently, the compelling merit of what you have written added to your own signal achievements prior to and during the war have created an expectancy.'

Winston, Clementine and Mary Churchill, accompanied by Maryott Whyte, on their way to the celebration of the Silver Jubilee of King George V and Queen Mary at Westminster Hall, London, 9 May 1935

On this day, Mary was 'thirteen and much excited'. Maryott Whyte (or 'Cousin Moppet') was Clementine's cousin. A trained Norland nurse, she came to look after the Churchill children after the untimely death of Marigold in 1921. Mary spoke extremely fondly of Whyte, calling her 'the guardian angel of my childhood'.

After the general election in 1935, Churchill's name did not appear on the list of new ministers. 'This was to me a pang, and in a way, an insult,' he later wrote. 'There was much mockery in the press. I do not pretend that, thirsting to get on the move, I was not distressed.'

Churchill leaves his Conservative constituency party offices, Epping, on general election day, 14 November 1935
Many, including the Germans, thought that Stanley Baldwin would make Churchill part of the new Cabinet after the 1935 general election. From Berlin, Gerard Muirhead-Gould of Naval Intelligence wrote: 'The Germans fear, and I hope, you will be 1st Lord – or Minister of Defence! Please don't give me away.'

The Conservatives won with an overwhelming majority and Churchill retained his own seat with an increased majority. The newspaper magnate Max Beaverbrook, a close friend, pointed out to Churchill: 'Well, you're finished now.

Baldwin has so good a majority that he will be able to do without you.'

Thomas Jones, a member of Baldwin's Cabinet, complimented the Prime Minister for having 'kept clear of Winston's enthusiasm for ships and guns'. However, Baldwin's explanation of this decision not to appoint Churchill was more insightful: 'I feel we should not give him a post at this stage. Anything he undertakes he puts his heart and soul into. If there is going to be a war – and no one can say that there is not – we must keep him fresh to be our war Prime Minister.'

Churchill at Euston Station, where he named a new locomotive *Royal Naval Division*, with General Sir Ian Hamilton and the train's driver, London, 5 June 1937

Churchill had founded the Royal Naval Division at the beginning of the First World War, due to the surplus of reservists in the Royal Navy. Often referred to as 'Winston's Little Army', this infantry division first saw action at Antwerp in 1914. In 1937, the name *Royal Naval Division* was given to a new locomotive of the London, Midland and Scottish Railway (L.M.S.). At Euston, Churchill admired the train driver's peaked cap, greasy and time-worn, and tried it on. They talked on, and Churchill walked off, still wearing the locomotive headgear. A newspaper wrote of the event: 'Perhaps it was not wholly intentional that he acquired an addition to his hat collection this week. He had to christen a new L. M. S. express locomotive of a class designated by military names. Mr. Churchill alone could fittingly act in the name of the Royal Naval Division, with its memories of Antwerp in the war and it was a happy coincidence that on the footplate was a driver who had served with Mr. Churchill in the war... But Driver Sparkes did not return the compliment by gracing the footplate in Mr Churchill's Homberg!'

At the 1937 party conference, Chamberlain said that 'until the world recovers some of its sanity, there can be no halt in the process of rearming this country'.

Churchill signs autographs at the Conservative Party Conference, Scarborough, 7 October 1937
The 1937 conference was Neville Chamberlain's first as Prime Minister and party leader. '[N]on-combatants, men, women and children, are being killed and mutilated by the action of aerial weapons,' he said of wars in Spain and China. 'Cruelty and barbarity... are the inevitable accompaniments of modern warfare. The real crime against humanity ... lies in having to resort to force at all, in contradiction of engagements solemnly entered into, without even an attempt to settle differences by peaceful discussion and negotiation.'

Churchill advocated the current foreign policy: 'I used to come here year after year when we had some differences between ourselves about rearmament ... So I thought it would only be right that I should come here when we are all agreed.'

Churchill opens the fifth National Book Fair at Dorland Hall, London, 8 November 1937
'The glory of literature in any free country is its variety, and the most fertile means from which happiness may be derived in life is from variety,' Churchill said at the opening of the fifth National Book Fair in London. 'The issues in the world today are such that readers should be on their guard against any attempt to warp their intellects or to narrow or enfeeble their judgement by tendentious literature with facts increasingly coloured and statistics ever more carefully selected. The ordinary man and woman in the age in which we move has to have a new vigilance and to be alive to new perils, to see that they are not being sucked in by propaganda.'

Churchill walks down Whitehall with Lord Halifax, the Foreign Secretary, London, 29 March 1938

On 13 March 1938, Adolf Hitler achieved the Anschluss, annexing Austria to Germany. Lord Halifax, the Foreign Secretary, had visited Hitler in November 1937. On his return, he had reported to the Cabinet that 'he had encountered friendliness and a desire for good relations' and that he would expect 'a beaver-like persistence' from Germany 'in pressing their aims in Central Europe, but not in a form to give others cause – or probably occasion – to interfere'. In conclusion, he said that Hitler 'strongly criticized widespread talk of an imminent catastrophe and did not consider that the world was in a dangerous state'.

On 14 March 1938, Churchill told the House of Commons: 'There is only one choice open, not only to us but to other countries, either to submit like Austria, or else take effective measures while time remains to ward off danger, and if it cannot be warded off to cope with it ... How many friends will be alienated, how many potential allies shall we see go one by one down the grisly gulf? How many times will bluff succeed until behind bluff ever gathering forces have accumulated in reality? ...Where are we going to be two years hence, for instance, when the German Army will certainly be much larger than the French Army, and when all the small nations will have fled from Geneva to pay homage to the ever waxing powers of the Nazi system, and to make the best terms that they can for themselves?'

'My good friends, for the second time in our history, a British Prime Minister has returned from Germany bringing peace with honour. I believe it is peace for our time,' said Neville Chamberlain on 30 September 1938. 'Go home and get a nice quiet sleep.'

Neville Chamberlain returns from the Munich Conference, Heston Aerodrome, 30 September 1938

On 29 September 1938, the Munich Conference resulted in Hitler, Chamberlain, and the Italian and French leaders Mussolini and Daladier signing an agreement that, among other things, permitted Germany to annex parts of Czechoslovakia. On 30 September, a jubilant Chamberlain landed at Heston. 'The settlement of the Czechoslovakian problem, which has now been achieved, is in my view only the prelude to a larger settlement in which all Europe may find peace. This morning I had another talk with the German Chancellor, Herr Hitler, and here is the paper which bears his name upon it as well as mine,' he said to the gathered crowd. 'We regard the agreement signed last night and the Anglo-German naval agreement as symbolic of the desire of our two peoples never to go to war with one another again.'

On 5 October, Churchill warned the House of Commons: 'Do not suppose that this is the end. This is only the beginning of the reckoning. This is only the first sip, the first foretaste of a bitter cup which will be proffered to us year by year unless, by a supreme recovery of moral health and martial vigour, we arise again and take our stand for freedom as in the olden time.' A year later, Hitler denounced the Munich Agreement as just a 'scrap of paper'.

On 1 September 1939, Germany invaded Poland. That day, Chamberlain finally asked Churchill to join the Cabinet as First Lord of the Admiralty. On 3 September, Britain declared war on Germany.

Winston and Clementine at Chartwell, 1939

In the 1930s, the Churchills were spending more and more time at their country home, an hour from London. 'Chartwell was ever and always the focus of Winston and Clementine's family and social life,' their daughter Mary recalled. As the decade wore on, their visitors included 'courageous men from the armed forces and the administration who, seeing the danger to the country, took risks with their own careers and reputations to fuel the power of seemingly the one man who could do something to awaken Britain both to the dangers in Europe... and the weak state of this country's defences.'

In 1939, the Churchills would spend their last months of peace at Chartwell for years to come.

7

*The
Second
World War:
1939–1945*

On hearing of Churchill's appointment as First Lord, the Board of Admiralty signalled to the Fleet: 'Winston is back.' In a broadcast on 1 October 1939, Churchill said: 'Here I am in the same post as I was in 25 years ago. Rough times lie ahead...'

Churchill arrives at the Admiralty as the newly appointed First Lord on 4 September 1939, the day after the outbreak of war. At his feet are two despatch boxes and a canvas bag containing his gas mask

The day Britain declared war on Germany, Churchill told the House of Commons: 'Outside, the storms of war may blow and the lands may be lashed with the fury of its gales, but in our own hearts this Sunday morning there is peace. Our hands may be active, but our consciences are at rest. This is not a question of fighting for Danzig or fighting for Poland. We are fighting to save the whole world from the pestilence of Nazi tyranny and in defence of all that is most sacred to man. This is no war for domination or imperial aggrandisement or material gain; no war to shut any country out of its sunlight and means of progress. It is a war...to establish, on impregnable rocks, the rights of the individual, and it is a war to establish and revive the stature of man.'

Churchill began his work at the same desk in the same room that he had occupied between 1911 and 1915, when he had last held the post of First Lord of the Admiralty. He would now be working closely with First Sea Lord Sir Dudley Pound, whom he had recently criticized over the disposition of the Mediterranean fleet.

Churchill addresses the crew of HMS *Exeter*, Plymouth, 14 February 1940

Churchill boarded the cruiser *Exeter* on her return to Plymouth following her actions with German pocket battleship *Admiral Graf Spee* at the Battle of the River Plate, off the east coast of South America. *Admiral Graf Spee* had sunk a number of British merchant vessels in the South Atlantic. On the morning of 13 December 1939, she attacked *Exeter*, which returned fire along with *Ajax* and *Achilles*. This action resulted in the death of 64 officers and men on board *Exeter*.

Surgeon-Lieutenant Roger Lancashire, who attended the dying and injured, remembered: 'On deck I had never seen anything like it before: the immaculate *Exeter* I'd known for three years was an absolute shambles.'

The *Graf Spee* sought sanctuary in Montevideo, the capital of neutral Uruguay. Three days later, Captain Hans Langsdorff, wrongly believing himself blockaded by overwhelming forces, scuttled his own ship.

In a radio broadcast, Churchill told the nation: 'This brilliant sea fight takes its place in our naval annals, and in a long, dark winter it warmed the cockles of the British hearts.'

On 10 May 1940, Churchill became Prime Minister and appointed himself Minister of Defence. His name is engraved on the ministerial despatch box in gold.

The despatch box marked 'War Office'
On 4 April 1940, it was announced that, as well as being First Lord of the Admiralty, Churchill was to head a committee whose job was to advise the War Cabinet regularly on the conduct of the war. On 9 April, Hitler invaded Denmark and Norway. After the failure of the British forces to save them, Chamberlain resigned as Prime Minister.

On 10 May 1940, after Lord Halifax, the Foreign Secretary, had stated his reluctance to take on the task, King George VI formally asked Churchill to form a government. The same day, Hitler ordered the invasion of Holland and Belgium. As Churchill began to formulate his Coalition Government, he felt that his moment had finally come: '...as I went to bed at about 3 a.m., I was conscious of a profound sense of relief. At last I had the authority to give directions over the whole scene. I felt as if I were walking with destiny, and that all my past life had been but a preparation for this hour and for this trial.'

Churchill's notes for his 'Finest Hour' speech, which he delivered twice on 18 June 1940: first to members of the House of Commons and later to the nation by means of the radio

Following Hitler's invasion of the Low Countries, Allied forces, including the BEF, were sent to the Belgian border to counter the advance. However, the real danger lay further south, as Panzer tank divisions crashed through the supposedly impenetrable Ardennes region, encircling the Allies. British troops were involved in a fighting retreat to the north coast where more than 338,000 Allied troops were evacuated from the piers and beaches of Dunkirk by ferries, fishing boats, yachts and naval vessels. In the meantime, Churchill's War Cabinet discussed the possibility of allowing Benito Mussolini to broker peace negotiations between Britain and Germany. Churchill rejected the idea, arguing that a negotiated peace with Germany would make Britain a slave state. When he stated his views to the wider Cabinet, they were received with a roar of support. On 17 June 1940, the French Prime Minister, Paul Reynaud, resigned and was replaced by Marshal Philippe Pétain, who sought an immediate armistice with Germany. France had been defeated; Britain, with her colonies and the dominions, now stood alone against Germany. In July 1940, in the skies above, the Battle of Britain began.

Upon this battle depends the
    survival of Christian civilization.

Upon it depends our own British life
    and the long continuity of our
    institutions, and our Empire.

The whole fury and might of the enemy
    must very soon be turned on us.

Hitler knows that we will hv to break
    us in this Island, or lose the war.

If we can stand up to him,
    all Europe may be freed,
        and the life of the world
            may move forward into the
                broad and sunlit uplands.

But if we fail,
    then the whole world,
        including the United States,
            and all that we have known and
                                cared for,
        will sink into the abyss of a
            new Dark Age
                made more sinister and
                    perhaps more prolonged by
                        the lights of perverted
                            Science.

Let us therefore brace ourselves to
    our duty, and so bear ourselves that
        if the British Empire and
            Commonwealth lasts for a
                thousand years, men will still
                    say,

'This was their finest hour'.

After Buckingham Palace was damaged in an air raid in September 1940, the Queen said, 'I'm glad we've been bombed, too. It makes me feel I can look those East End mothers in the face.'

King George VI and Queen Elizabeth, accompanied by Churchill, inspect the damage to Buckingham Palace on the morning after the building was hit in an air raid, 13 September 1940

With the death toll in London standing at a thousand a week, Churchill defiantly broadcast this message on 11 September 1940: 'These cruel, wanton, indiscriminate bombings of London are, of course, a part of Hitler's invasion plans. He hopes, by killing large numbers of civilians, and women and children, that he will terrorize and cow the people of this mighty imperial city... Little does he know the spirit of the British nation, or the tough fibre of the Londoners... He has lighted a fire which will burn with a steady and consuming flame until the last vestiges of Nazi tyranny have been burnt out.'

Winston and Clementine return from inspecting the damage caused by multiple air raids on the docks of the River Thames, London, 25 September 1940

By 22 September 1940 the RAF had defeated the Luftwaffe in the Battle of Britain and retained air superiority. This forced Hitler to cancel his plans for the invasion of Britain, code-named Operation Sea Lion. In early September he had changed tactics and begun to bomb British towns and cities, particularly targeting munition factories and the major docks. Churchill made it his job to visit the places most affected by these air raids and Clementine sometimes accompanied him. They were both visibly moved by the extent of the destruction.

Churchill waits for a train at St Andrews station after inspecting General Sikorski's Polish troops in Scotland, 23 October 1940

In October 1940, Churchill made an inspection of troops and coastal fortifications in Scotland. He was photographed at St Andrews station, wearing his flat-topped bowler hat (known as a bowker), oblivious to the commotion caused by his presence.

Scotland was completely unprotected from the threat of German attack from Norway and in August 1940 Polish troops arrived to help in her defence. They received a warm welcome and immediately set to work defending their new homeland. There was little military infrastructure to accommodate them and they were left largely to their own devices. They soon established their own camps, built sea defences and constantly patrolled the coastlines.

Roosevelt and Churchill would not meet in person until August 1941, but in January of that year they began a close correspondence, going on to exchange 1,700 letters before Roosevelt's death in 1945.

Letter from Franklin D. Roosevelt, the President of the United States, to Churchill, 20 January 1941
Roosevelt's letter to Churchill features lines from the poem 'The Building of the Ship', by the nineteenth-century American poet Henry Wadsworth Longfellow:

'Sail on, Oh Ship of State!
Sail on, Oh Union strong and great.
Humanity with all its fears,
With all the hopes of future years
Is hanging breathless on thy fate.'

In his letter Roosevelt also mentions Wendell Wilkie, who had been his Republican opponent in the recent presidential election but whom he found congenial and interesting for his international views. Wilkie hand-delivered this letter to Churchill who, desperate for American support in the war effort, told Roosevelt that it was 'an inspiration' and that he would have it framed. Indeed, the letter hung for many years at Chartwell.

Churchill went on to share the letter with the British people. In his broadcast of 27 April 1941, he said: 'Last time I spoke to you I quoted the lines of Longfellow which President Roosevelt had written out for me in his own hand. I have some other lines which are less well known but which seem apt and appropriate to our fortunes tonight, and I believe they will be so judged wherever the English language is spoken or the flag of freedom flies:

'...And not by eastern windows only,
When daylight comes, comes in the light;
In front the sun climbs slow, how slowly,
But westward, look, the land is bright.'

Churchill was quoting 'Say Not The Struggle Naught Availeth', by the English poet Arthur Hugh Clough.

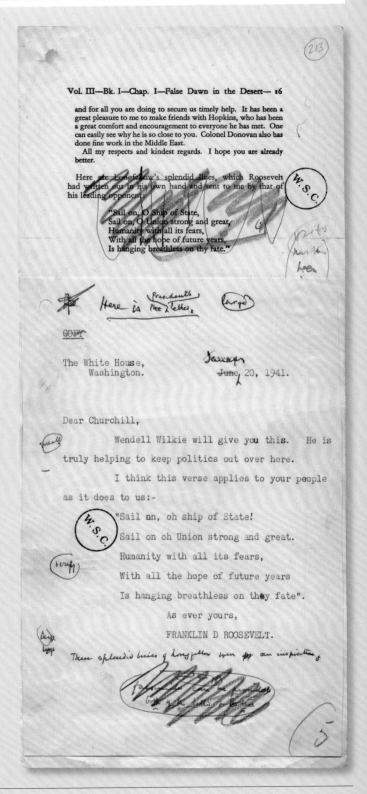

A breakdown of Churchill's expenditure on wines, spirits, cigars and cigarettes between October 1939 and March 1941

During the 'Phoney War' in the months immediately after the invasion of Poland, Churchill's expenditure on wines, spirits and cigars actually fell. However, the records show that after May 1940, when he became Prime Minister, his consumption leapt, peaking in February 1941.

Churchill would usually start the day with what his daughter called the 'Daddy Cocktail', a drink that contained Johnnie Walker whisky and soda. This was a habit he had picked up as a young man while serving in India, where the water wasn't drinkable without alcohol.

In 1899, while Churchill was covering the Second Boer War as the war correspondent for the *Morning Post*, he reportedly went to the frontline with 36 bottles of wine, 18 bottles of scotch and 6 bottles of brandy.

Churchill's love of Pol Roger champagne dated back to a lunch given by the British Ambassador to France shortly after the liberation of Paris in the First World War. Here, he had met Odette Pol Roger, who was to become a great friend. Pol Roger created their Prestige Cuvée in homage to Churchill, mindful of the qualities that he sought in his champagne: robustness, a full-bodied character and relative maturity.

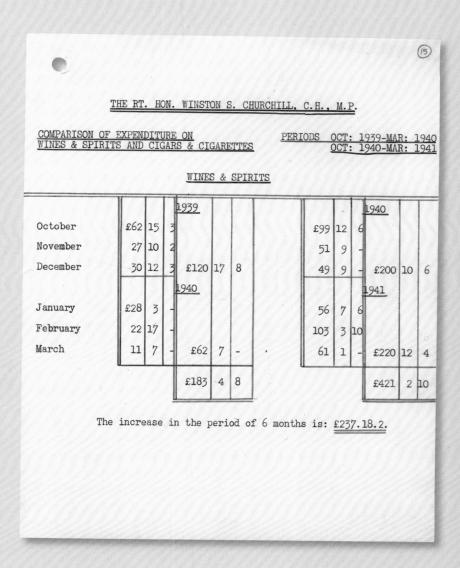

(15)

THE RT. HON. WINSTON S. CHURCHILL, C.H., M.P.

COMPARISON OF EXPENDITURE ON WINES & SPIRITS AND CIGARS & CIGARETTES
PERIODS OCT: 1939–MAR: 1940 OCT: 1940–MAR: 1941

WINES & SPIRITS

	1939					1940			
October	£62	15	3			£99	12	6	
November	27	10	2			51	9	-	
December	30	12	3	£120 17 8		49	9	-	£200 10 6
	1940					1941			
January	£28	3	-			56	7	6	
February	22	17				103	3	10	
March	11	7	-	£62 7 -		61	1	-	£220 12 4
				£183 4 8					£421 2 10

The increase in the period of 6 months is: £237.18.2.

Churchill visits Bristol after the city is hit by a series of bombing raids, 14 April 1941

On 9 April 1941, it was officially announced that nearly 30,000 British civilians had been killed in air raids since the start of the war. In Bristol the two major dates of devastation were 11 and 12 April, when the city was hit by incendiary bombs that caused numerous fires and were designed to cause panic among the citizens. Following these bombings, which became known as the Good Friday Raids, the city's morale was at an all-time low. Churchill, realizing the depths of people's despair, visited the worst-affected areas and spoke warmly to those who had lost their homes.

General Hastings Ismay, who was with Churchill during this visit, later wrote to him: 'People were still being dug out, but there was no sign of a faltering anywhere. Only efficiency and resolution. At one of the rest centres at which you called, there was a poor old woman who had lost all her belongings sobbing her heart out. But as you entered, she took her handkerchief from her eyes and waved it madly shouting, "Hooray, hooray."'

When war was once again declared in September 1939, the Red Cross joined forces with the Order of St John and carried out everything from nursing and air-raid duties to searching for missing people and transporting the wounded.

Churchill contributes to the Red Cross Flag Day, 5 June 1941

Churchill was very aware of the tremendous work the Red Cross had done during the First World War. Their work during the Second World War was funded by the Duke of Gloucester's Red Cross and St John Appeal, which had raised over £54 million by 1946, in excess of £2 billion in modern terms.

On 22 June 1941, Germany invaded Russia, and despite their previous animosity, Britain rushed to Russia's aid. In October, the Red Cross and Order of St John started an 'Aid to Russia Fund', inviting Clementine to be Chairman of the Appeal Committee. It became known as 'Mrs Churchill's Aid to Russia Fund'.

C. R. ✓ ②

PRIME MINISTER.

I attach below an extract from a letter from Lord Halifax about a gift of cigars from Mr. Sam M. Kaplan of New York. These cigars have now arrived.

You will shortly be receiving another large consignment of cigars bought for you by subscribers to the Cuban newspaper "Bohemia" and also 2,400 cigars from the Cuban National Commission of Tobacco.

I have discussed with the Professor, and also with Lord Rothschild of M.I.5., the question of security and they both insist that however reputable the source from which the cigars come it is impossible to ensure that they are safe. It would be perfectly possible to insert a grain of deadly poison in, say, one cigar in fifty, and although Lord Rothschild can and will arrange for those that arrive to be

C. R. ③

x-rayed, he would only guarantee them as safe after when subjecting each one to a careful analysis. This could not be done without destroying the cigars.

The element of risk is slight in the case of Mr. Kaplan's cigars and all those sent from Cuba. Sir G. Ogilvie Forbes has vouched for the bona fides of the "Bohemia" and of the Cuban National Commission of Tobacco. Nevertheless, the proposal to make these gifts to you was/very widely advertised and (except in the case of Mr Kaplan) an enemy agent might have been able to suborn one of the men engaged in the rolling or packing of the cigars. Professor Lindemann and Lord Rothschild were strongly of the opinion that you ought not to smoke any cigars received from overseas while the war lasts. The Professor thought however that you might like to let them accumulate in a safe and dry place until after the war, when you would be might feel justified in taking the risk involved in smoking

---

Above: **A memo to Churchill from his assistant private secretary, John 'Jock' Colville, concerning the safety of consignments of cigars sent to the Prime Minister during wartime, 18 June 1941**

In April 1941, a large mahogany cabinet containing 2,400 fine cigars was presented to the British Ambassador in Cuba. Intended as a gift for Churchill from the Cuban National Commission for Tobacco, the cabinet and its contents caused concern among the Prime Minister's advisors, who feared that 'any noxious substance could have been added to the cigars during the process of manufacture'. When the cabinet finally arrived in Britain in August of that year, Churchill waited impatiently as rigorous tests (involving mice being injected with small samples of cigar) were carried out by MI5's biological experts. Only in September, once the mice were seen to have survived their injections, was Churchill allowed to enjoy his present.

Opposite: **On board HMS *Prince of Wales*, Churchill strokes Blackie, the ship's cat, August 1941**

In August 1941, Churchill set sail from Thurso, Scotland, for a meeting with Roosevelt in Placentia Bay, Newfoundland. On 10 August, both men with their ships' companies attended Divine Service on board the *Prince of Wales*. 'This service was felt by us all to be a deeply moving expression of the unity of faith of our two peoples, and none who took part in it will forget the spectacle presented that sunlit morning on the crowded quarterdeck – the symbolism of the Union Jack and the Stars and Stripes draped side by side on the pulpit...the close-packed ranks of British and American sailors, completely intermingled, sharing the same books and joining fervently together in the prayers and hymns familiar to both – *For Those in Peril on the Sea* and *Onward Christian Soldiers*. We ended with *O God, Our Help in Ages Past*,' Churchill recalled. 'Every word seemed to stir the heart. It was a great hour to live. Nearly half those who sang were soon to die.'

Churchill on board the
Prince of Wales, **7 August 1941**
While Churchill had thoroughly
enjoyed meeting Roosevelt for the first
time, not as much progress had been
made in their meeting as he had hoped.
The most important of the pledges that
the US had made was that she would
give aid to Russia 'on a gigantic scale',
which she would co-ordinate with
Britain. The US would also provide a
five-destroyer escort for every North
Atlantic convoy to Britain, as well
as a cruiser or other ships in order to
deliver bombers, though not as many
as Churchill wanted. The two leaders
agreed that both countries would
'respect the rights of all peoples to
choose the form of government under
which they live', in a document that
became known as the Atlantic Charter.

On 29 August, Churchill wrote
to his son Randolph: 'One is deeply
perplexed to know how the deadlock
is to be broken and the United States
brought boldly and honourably into
the war.' The next day, Churchill
spoke to the Canadian Prime Minister
Mackenzie King and other guests
at Chequers, the official country
residence of British Prime Ministers,
with some frustration about the US
not declaring war: 'Though we cannot
now be defeated, the war might drag
on for another four or five years, and
civilization and culture would be
wiped out.'

In May 1941, Churchill said of Liverpool: 'I see the damage done by the enemy attacks, but I also see the spirit of an unconquered people.'

Churchill speaks to dock workers during a morale-boosting tour of Liverpool, September 1941
Liverpool was of great importance in the war. The Battle of the Atlantic was co-ordinated from the Combined Operations Headquarters in Derby House and civilian and military supplies were brought into the city through the convoy system. The Mersey waterfront was vital for naval repairs and shipbuilding, making it a key target for German bombers. Keen to boost the morale of war-weary Liverpudlians, Churchill toured the city with Clementine. He spoke to dock workers having their lunch and asked: 'Are you managing to get plenty of food?' 'Aye, sir, we're doing grand, thank you,' was the reply.

Churchill walks amid the ruins of Coventry Cathedral, September 1941
Code named Operation Moonlight Sonata, the raid carried out by 515 German
bombers on the evening of 14 November 1940 was intended to destroy Coventry's
industrial infrastructure. High-explosive bombs knocked out water, gas and
electricity supplies and cratered the roads, while waves of incendiary bombs
caused 200 fires across the city. By 8 pm the cathedral was on fire and more bombs
were dropped on this beautiful 14th-century building before the raid reached
its climax around midnight. In one night, 568 people were killed and more than
4,300 homes destroyed, marking a new level of destruction.

Left: A year after the Battle of Britain, Churchill, wearing the uniform of an Air Commodore, and Clementine meet the pilots of the No. 615 Fighter Squadron, 25 September 1941 In August 1940, Churchill had told the House of Commons and, in a broadcast, the whole nation: 'The gratitude of every home in our Island, in our Empire, and indeed throughout the world, except in the abodes of the guilty, goes out to the British airmen who, undaunted by odds, unwearied in their constant challenge and mortal danger, are turning the tide of the world war by their prowess and by their devotion. Never in the field of human conflict was so much owed by so many to so few.'

Opposite: Churchill attends an England vs. Scotland football match at Wembley Stadium, 4 October 1941
While normal Football League games were suspended for the duration of the war, the Football Association grouped teams into regional divisions for the Wartime League. Soon after the start of the Blitz, the FA relaxed their ban on Sunday football in order to boost morale and provide recreation.

In October 1941, Churchill attended a match between fierce rivals England and Scotland, with a crowd of 65,000. In the previous encounter, played in Glasgow in May that year, Scotland had won 3-1. At Wembley, England got their revenge, winning 2-0.

Above: Winston is seen off by Mary, HMS *Duke of York*, 13 December 1941
On 7 December 1941, Japan attacked Pearl Harbor in Hawaii. Two days later, off the coast of Malaya, Japanese fighter aircraft sank the British battleships *Repulse* and *Prince of Wales*. On 12 December 1941, Churchill set off for the US on the battleship *Duke of York* to discuss with Roosevelt what had now become a world war. 'No American will think it wrong of me if I proclaim to have the United States at our side was to me the greatest joy. I could not foretell the course of events. I do not pretend to have measured accurately the martial might of Japan, but now at this very moment I knew the United States was in the war, up to the neck and in to the death. So we had won after all!' Churchill later wrote: 'We had won the war. England would live; Britain would live; the Commonwealth of Nations and the Empire would live. How long the war would last or in what fashion it would end no man could tell, nor did I at this moment care. Once again in our long Island history we should emerge, however mauled or mutilated, safe and victorious. We should not be wiped out. Our history would not come to an end. We might not even have to die as individuals. Hitler's fate was sealed. Mussolini's fate was sealed. As for the Japanese, they would be ground to powder...'

Churchill spent Christmas 1941 at the White House, working out a global war strategy with Roosevelt that much to his relief prioritized the Anglo-American defeat of Germany before the defeat of Japan.

Opposite: **Churchill photographed by Yousuf Karsh, Ottawa, 30 December 1941**
As well as visiting the US in late 1941, Churchill went to Canada to see Prime Minister Mackenzie King, whom he much admired. In Ottawa he delivered a speech to Canadian MPs and senators, in which he referred to a comment made by Philippe Pétain, who was convinced that Britain would be as easily invaded by Germany as France had been: 'In three weeks England will have her neck wrung like a chicken.' Churchill responded: 'Some chicken! Some neck!' Later in the speech, he proudly spoke of the people of London: '...look at what they have stood up to. Grim and gay with their cry "We can take it", and their wartime mood of "What is good enough for anybody is good enough for us"...Hitler and his Nazi gang have sown the wind; let them reap the whirlwind.'

Afterwards, Churchill reluctantly agreed to pose for the then little-known photographer Yousuf Karsh. Karsh set out to create an iconic shot, but without the iconic cigar. He approached Churchill with an ashtray, but Churchill refused to put down his cigar. Karsh recalled: 'I stepped towards him and, without premeditation, but ever so respectfully, I said, "Forgive me, sir" and plucked the cigar out of his mouth. By the time I got back to my camera, he looked so belligerent he could have devoured me. It was at that instant that I took the photograph.'

Above: **Churchill at the White House with Diana Hopkins, the daughter of Harry Hopkins, a personal envoy of Roosevelt's, and Roosevelt's dog Fala, c. 3 January 1942**
Churchill wrote of the Christmas festivities in Washington: 'The President and I went to church together on Christmas Day, and I found peace in the simple service and enjoyed singing the well-known hymns, and one, *O Little Town of Bethlehem*, I had never heard before. Certainly there was much to fortify the faith of all who believe in the moral governance of the universe.'

In this photograph, Churchill is seen wearing one of his favourite outfits, a one-piece garment with a zip fastener known as a 'siren suit', which had the particular advantage of being able to be put on in a minute.

Churchill was not happy when he saw a cartoon that he interpreted as an attack on his government for allowing sailors to die so that oil companies could profit. In fact, it was intended as a patriotic warning not to waste petrol.

'The price of petrol has been increased by one penny: Official', by Philip Zec, *Daily Mirror*, 6 March 1942
Philip Zec had intended his cartoon about the price of petrol to be seen as a warning not to waste fuel, as its shortage was costing sailors' lives. Churchill's misunderstanding of Zec's intention was shared by Home Secretary Herbert Morrison, who disparaged the cartoon as 'wicked...Goebbels at his best' and Cecil Thomas, the editor of the *Daily Mirror*, as 'very unpatriotic'. An MI5 investigation of Zec, called for

by Churchill, disclosed nothing other than the cartoonist's left-wing political sympathies, but the high-profile negative reaction to this drawing almost led to the forced closure of the *Mirror*. Zec was labelled a traitor.

Three years later, however, Morrison had to eat his words when Zec published a popular cartoon for VE day. It showed a badly wounded soldier offering a laurel branch symbolizing victory and peace in Europe, with the caption 'Here you are. Don't lose it again!'

<u>Below:</u> **Churchill and Stalin at the Kremlin, Moscow, 16 August 1942**
On 10 August 1942 Churchill set off from Cairo to Moscow by plane to tell Stalin personally that there could be no 'Second Front' at that time. He had mixed feelings about being in Russia: 'I pondered on my mission to this sullen, sinister Bolshevik State I had once tried so hard to strangle at its birth, and which, until Hitler appeared, I had regarded as the mortal foe of civilized freedom.' However, he soon wrote to the War Cabinet and Roosevelt of a surprisingly agreeable encounter: 'I had a very good interpreter, and was able to talk much more easily. The greatest goodwill prevailed and for the first time we got on to easy and friendly terms. I feel that I have established a personal relationship which will be helpful.'

On 17 August, in a broadcast back to Moscow from Cairo, Churchill said: 'We are full of determination to continue the struggle hand in hand, whatever sufferings and hardships may await us, and to continue the struggle hand in hand as comrades and brothers until the last vestiges of the Hitlerite *régime* are turned to dust, remaining in the memory as an example and a warning for the future.'

<u>Above:</u> **Churchill with Victor Lampson, the son of the British Ambassador to Egypt, at the British Embassy in Cairo, 8 August 1942**
Churchill had flown to Egypt to appoint a new Middle East Commander, General Alexander, as well as a new Commander of the Eighth Army. The intention was for General William Gott to be given the latter post, but he had unfortunately been killed the day before when his aeroplane was shot down. Instead, Churchill appointed General Bernard Montgomery.

Sir Alexander Cadogan of the Foreign Office, who accompanied Churchill, described the event in his diary: '[T]he PM appeared in his rompers and what he calls his 10-gallon hat – a sort of Mexican affair...after that, the Army photographers and cinema operators were admitted to the garden to photograph Winston and [South African General Jan] Smuts playing with baby Victor! What England will think when the film is released, I really cannot imagine.'

After a series of losses for the Allies, the Eighth Army defeated Rommel's forces in Egypt in November 1942. 'We have victory – a remarkable and definite victory,' Churchill said.

General Alexander's telegram to Churchill regarding Allied success in North Africa, 4 November 1942

In reply to General Alexander's telegram, shown here, Churchill wrote: 'I send you my heartfelt congratulations on the splendid feat of arms achieved by the Eighth Army under the command of your brilliant lieutenant, Montgomery, in the Battle of Egypt. Although the fruits may take some days or even weeks to gather, it is evident that an event of the first magnitude has occurred'.

A week later, he spoke confidently at the Lord Mayor's Day luncheon at the Mansion House, London: 'We have victory – a remarkable and definite victory. The bright gleam has caught the helmets of our soldiers, and warmed and cheered all our hearts.

'This battle was not fought for the sake of gaining positions or so many square miles of desert territory. General Alexander and General Montgomery fought it with one single idea. They meant to destroy the armed force of the enemy, and to destroy it at the place where the disaster would be most far-reaching and irrecoverable ... I recall to you some lines of Byron, which seem to me to fit the event, the hour, and the theme:

'Millions of tongues record thee, and anew
Their children's lips shall echo them, and say –
'Here, where the sword united nations drew,
Our countrymen were warring on that day!'
And this is much, and all which will not pass away.'

(25)

IZ 2047

TOO 0950z/4

TOR 1130z/4

MOST
SECRET CYPHER TELEGRAM

MOST IMMEDIATE

PRIME MINISTER'S
PERSONAL TELEGRAM

(7)

From:- Middle East

To:- Air Ministry

THE CHARTWELL TRUST

SERIAL No. T. 1422/2

No.CS/1647 4/11/42

Personal for Prime Minister from General Alexander.

Copy to C.I.G.S.

After twelve days of heavy and violent fighting 8th Army has inflicted a severe defeat on the enemy's German and Italian forces under Rommel's command in Egypt. The enemy's front has broken and British armoured formations in strength have passed through and are operating in the enemy's rear areas. Such portions of the enemy's forces as can get away are in full retreat and are being harassed by our armoured and mobile forces and by our Air Forces. Other enemy divisions are still in position endeavouring to stave off defeat and these are likely to be surrounded and cut off.

The R.A.F. has throughout given superb support to the land battle and are bombing the enemy's retreating columns incessantly.

Fighting continues.

T.O.O. 0950z/4

Circulation
The King
Brig. Jacob
C.A.S.
C.I.G.S.
First Sea Lord
Defence Cmttee. } Defence Registry arranging.
War Cabinet }

Churchill, aged 67, crosses a greased log at an infantry training battle course, Kent, 20 November 1942
The day after visiting troops training in Kent, Churchill wrote to the Secretary of State for War, Sir James Grigg: 'I was shocked to hear yesterday, when visiting the 53rd Division, that an Army Council instruction had been issued three days ago ordering the immediate removal of all regimental shoulder-badges... There is no doubt that it will be extremely unpopular and tend to destroy that regimental *esprit de corps* upon which all armies worthy of the name are founded... I hope you will give directions to cancel the instruction before great harm is done.'

Churchill and Roosevelt visit Shangri-La (now known as Camp David), Maryland, May 1943
In May 1943, Churchill attended the Trident Conference in Washington. On 19 May, he made a speech to both Houses of Congress in which he stressed that the main fighting on land was still being borne at great cost on the Eastern Front by the Soviet Army. He was convinced that, despite the victory in Tunisia, the final triumph would only come after battles as difficult as those that had preceded the pivotal Battle of Gettysburg in the American Civil War.

Churchill dictated notes and letters whenever he had the chance, be it while travelling on a train through England or taking a bath at the White House.

Opposite: Churchill dictates to his secretary Kathleen Hill (out of shot) on a train journey to the south-east of England, 1943
During one visit to the White House, Churchill emerged wrapped in a big towel after a morning spent dictating from the bathtub. 'He walked into his adjoining bedroom, followed by me, notebook in hand,' Patrick Kinna, a stenographer, recalled. '[He] continued to dictate while pacing up and down the enormous room. Eventually the towel fell to the ground ... Suddenly President Roosevelt entered the bedroom and saw the British Prime Minister completely naked ... WSC, never being lost for words, said, "You see Mr. President, I have nothing to conceal from you."'

Above: Churchill reaches the US, giving his famous 'V-for-Victory' sign to British sailors and airmen who had crossed the Atlantic with him, May 1943
Churchill first promoted the idea of using the V-for-Victory sign to inspire and unite the Allied countries in a broadcast on 19 July 1941: 'The V sign is the symbol of the unconquerable will of the occupied territories and a portent of the fate awaiting Nazi tyranny. So long as the peoples continue to refuse all collaboration with the invader it is sure that his cause will perish and that Europe will be liberated.' Walls chalked with 'Vs' and hand gestures could soon be seen all over Europe, especially in German-occupied cities.

Left: Churchill reaches out to a young fan from the back of a train to Niagara Falls, Canada, 12 August 1943
In August 1943, Churchill went to Canada for the Quebec Conference with Roosevelt and the Allied Chiefs of Staff. He took the train from Halifax, Nova Scotia, and was met by crowds at every station, because there were rumours that someone famous was on board – some said it was the Pope, others Stalin, but all were delighted that it was Churchill.

He had first visited Niagara Falls in 1900 and been highly impressed. By 1943, his enthusiam seemed to be waning. Asked if the falls had changed, he said: 'Well, the principle still seems the same. The water still keeps falling over.'

Below: Churchill on board HMS *Renown* with his daughter Sarah, First Sea Lord Sir John Cunningham and his doctor Lord Moran, en route to Alexandria, November 1943
On 11 November 1943 Churchill boarded the battleship *Renown* at Plymouth, feeling ill as a result of inoculations for cholera and typhoid. During their first day at sea, a naval officer calculated that Churchill had travelled 111,000 miles by sea and air since September 1939. By 1941, Sarah's marriage to the actor Vic Oliver had deteriorated and she joined the Women's Auxiliary Air Force (WAAF), becoming her father's aide-de-camp on his travels.

Opposite: Churchill is given a standing ovation by troops at a Roman theatre in Carthage, Tunisia, 1 June 1943
'The sense of victory was in the air,' Churchill recalled of his visit to Carthage. 'The whole of North Africa was cleared of the enemy. A quarter of a million prisoners were cooped in our cages. Everyone was very proud and delighted. There is no doubt that people like winning very much. I addressed many thousand soldiers at Carthage in the ruins of an immense amphitheatre. Certainly the hour and the setting lent themselves to oratory. I have no idea what I said, but the whole audience clapped and cheered as doubtless their predecessors of two thousand years ago had done as they watched gladiatorial combats.'

Malta had been a base for British submarines and aircraft that attacked the Axis lines of supply to Libya. In retaliation, in the spring of 1942, the Axis began a siege of annihilation. Malta never gave in, and the island was uniquely awarded the George Cross for its courage.

Below: **Churchill walks amid the destruction of Malta, which had been the target of intense aerial bombardment for over two years, 19 November 1943**
On 21 November 1943, after his visit to Malta, Churchill sent a telegram to Clementine. He used code names – the telegram was addressed from 'Colonel Warden to Mrs Warden'. In it, Churchill wrote: 'Have had for five days bad cold on chest now definitely mastered. This and bad weather decided me to go on in ship and am just reaching Alexandria after safe

Above: **Roosevelt and Churchill with General and Madame Chiang Kai-shek, Cairo, 25 November 1943**
At the Cairo Conference held in November 1943, Churchill, Roosevelt and Chinese leader Chiang Kai-shek met to discuss Japan and post-war Asia. 'I got on excellently with Madame Chiang Kai Shek,' Churchill wrote to Clementine, 'and I withdraw all the unfavourable remarks which I may have made about her.'

Discovering that Roosevelt had never seen the Sphinx or the Pyramids, Churchill arranged a visit there with his daughter Sarah. She wrote to her mother: '[T]he President was charming – simple and enthusiastic. I think he enjoyed himself – I think he enjoyed the trouble Papa took.'

voyage. We have been handed on from point to point by air cover and seapower without any molestation. Am still grieving over Leros etc [where German forces had captured 5,000 British soldiers, their first success since their defeat at El Alamein] ... Had great welcome from workmen in Malta Dockyard. Love from Sarah and me.'

<u>Above:</u> **Churchill wears a Persian lambswool hat and the uniform of an Air Commodore of the Royal Air Force while leaving the British Legation, Tehran, November 1943**
On 27 November 1943, Churchill and Roosevelt flew separately from Cairo to Tehran to meet Stalin. The next day, 'The Big Three' held a conference in which it was agreed that Operation Overlord, the invasion of Europe, would be launched in May 1944. The discussions carried on into a dinner, at which Churchill told Stalin: 'We are the trustees for the peace of the world. If we fail there will be perhaps a hundred years of chaos.... There is more than merely keeping the peace. The three Powers should guide the future of the world. I do not want to enforce any system on other nations. I ask for freedom and for the right of all nations to develop as they like.' Churchill then raised a toast 'to the Proletarian masses'. Stalin mischievously replied by raising his glass 'to the Conservative Party'.

On 30 November, while in Tehran, Churchill celebrated his 69th birthday. After the conferences and accompanied by Sarah, he travelled to Tunis, where he fell seriously ill with pneumonia. She recalled his words to her at that time: 'If I die, don't worry – the war is won.'

At the Tehran Conference, Stalin, unsure of Allied commitment to the Second Front, requested that a commander be appointed within a week. Churchill and Roosevelt agreed on Eisenhower as the Supreme Commander of the Allied Expeditionary Force.

Churchill fires a Tommy gun at a US Army Air Force base in Britain, after inspecting troops who would be taking part in D-Day. Behind him, also firing, is US General Dwight D. 'Ike' Eisenhower, 23 March 1944

Eisenhower was appointed as the Supreme Commander of the Allied Expeditionary Force in December 1943. His strength was considered to be strategy, so Montgomery was nominated as ground commander. The Thompson machine gun, better known as the Tommy gun, was introduced in the US in the 1920s. It was much sought after in the Prohibition Era, especially by criminals, who named it the 'Chicago Typewriter'. It was favoured by both criminals and soldiers for its compactness and high volume of fire, 600–725 rounds per minute.

Letter from King George VI to Churchill, 2 June 1944

On 30 May 1944, Churchill met with King George VI to discuss D-Day. The next day, the King wrote to Churchill that 'it would not be right for either you or I to be where we planned' on D-Day. They met again on 1 June. The next day, the King wrote again:

My dear Winston,
I want to make one more appeal to you not to go to sea on D day. Please consider my own position. I am a younger man than you, I am a sailor [George VI had seen action at the Battle of Jutland] *& as King I am the head of all three Services. There is nothing I would like better than to go to sea but I have agreed to stop at home; is it fair that you should then do exactly what I should have liked to do myself? You said yesterday afternoon that it would be a fine thing for the King to lead his troops into battle, as in old days; if the King cannot do this, it does not seem to me right that his Prime Minister should take his place.*

Then there is your own position; you will see very little, you will run a considerable risk, you will be inaccessible at a critical time when vital decisions might have to be taken, & however unobtrusive you may be, your mere presence on board is bound to be a very heavy additional responsibility to the Admiral & Captain.

As I said in my previous letter, your being there would add immeasurably to my own anxieties, & your going without consulting your colleagues in the Cabinet would put them in a very difficult position which they would justifiably resent.

I ask you most earnestly to consider the whole question again & not let your personal wishes, which I very well understand, lead you to depart from your own high standard of duty to the State.'

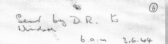

3 June, 1944.

Sir,

I must excuse myself for not having answered Your Majesty's letter earlier. It caught me just as I was leaving by the train and I have been in constant movement ever since. I had a despatch rider standing by in order to take it to you tonight.

Sir, I cannot really feel that the first paragraph of your letter takes sufficient account of the fact that there is absolutely no comparison in the British Constitution between a Sovereign and a subject. If Your Majesty had gone, as you desire, on board one of your ships in this bombarding action, it would have required the Cabinet approval beforehand and I am very much inclined to think, as I told you, that the Cabinet would have advised most strongly against

- 2 -

Your Majesty going.

On the other hand, as Prime Minister and Minister of Defence I ought to be allowed to go where I consider it necessary to the discharge of my duty, and I do not admit that the Cabinet have any right to put restrictions on my freedom of movement. I rely on my own judgment, invoked in many serious matters, as to what are the proper limits of risk which a person who discharges my duties is entitled to run. I must most earnestly ask Your Majesty that no principle shall be laid down which inhibits my freedom of movement when I judge it necessary to acquaint myself with conditions in the various theatres of war. Since Your Majesty does me the honour to be so much concerned about my personal safety on this occasion, I must defer to Your Majesty's wishes and indeed commands. It is a great comfort to me to know that they arise from Your Majesty's desire to continue me in your service. Though I regret that I cannot go, I am deeply grateful to Your Majesty for the motives

- 3 -

which have guided Your Majesty in respect of

Your Majesty's humble and devoted Servant and Subject,

Churchill's response to George VI's letter (see previous page), 3 June 1944

In the letter shown here, Churchill reluctantly gave in to the King's wish for him not to participate in the Normandy landings. The original date set for D-Day was 5 June 1944, but due to bad weather the operation was postponed until the following day. Flight Lieutenant Alec Blythe remembered meeting the Royal Engineers he was to drop on D-Day: 'They seemed jolly nice chaps. However, when they came up to the Dakota on the night of the operation with blackened faces they looked a fearsome lot. One pulled out his dagger and said that it was going to find a German that night. I was rather glad they were on our side.'

Clementine wrote to her husband on 5 June: 'I feel so much for you at this agonizing moment – so full of suspense, which prevents me from rejoicing over Rome [which had just been liberated]! I look forward to seeing you at dinner – Write a nice letter to the poor King!' Later that night, Churchill went to the Map Room for a final look at the Allied and German dispositions. Clementine joined him there and he said to her: 'Do you realize that by the time you wake up in the morning, twenty thousand men may have been killed?'

By the evening of 5 June 1944, weather conditions had improved enough for D-Day to go ahead. Churchill telegraphed Stalin: 'Tonight we go. We are using 5,000 ships and have available 11,000 aircraft.'

COPY

(4)

PRIME MINISTER'S
PERSONAL TELEGRAM
SERIAL No. T. 1203/4.

PRIME MINISTER TO MARSHAL STALIN
Personal and Top Secret

Everything has started well. The mines, obstacles and land batteries have been largely overcome. The Air landings were very successful and on a large scale. Infantry landings are proceeding rapidly and many tanks and self-propelled guns are already ashore. Weather outlook moderate to good.

W.S.C.

6.6.44.

THE CHARTWELL TRUST

Churchill's telegram to Stalin, 6 June 1944

Able Seaman Ken Oakley, one of the thousands ready to go on D-Day, wrote: 'On the evening prior to the landings, the senior army officer gave us a briefing and I will always remember his final words: "Don't worry if all the first wave of you are killed," he said. "We shall simply pass over your bodies with more and more men." What a confident thought to go to bed on.'

The next day Churchill telegraphed Stalin of the operation's initial success (see left). Oakley described hitting the beachhead: 'At the order "Down ramp", we were all surging ashore...all around were craft beaching and chaos and gunfire was pouring down on us. We ran, under fire, up to the top of the beach where we went to ground....'

Commando Sergeant William Spearman recalled: 'There were bodies – dead bodies, living bodies. All the blood in the water made it look as though men were drowning in their own blood. That's how it looked.'

All Churchill's children served in the armed forces: by June 1944, his youngest daughter Mary had worked her way up to command an anti-aircraft crew in Kent.

Winston and Mary Churchill watch measures to combat German V-1 flying bombs, Kent, 30 June 1944
Mary Churchill had at first found it difficult to be in the Army: 'I was received pretty frostily as everyone expected you to be above yourself. But once they discovered you scrubbed as many, if not more, floors as they did, they accepted one.' On 30 June 1944, Winston and Clementine visited Mary's anti-aircraft battery in Kent from nearby Chartwell.

Churchill has his cigar re-lit by a French docker on a visit to inspect the damage to the port of Cherbourg, July 1944
Following D-Day, one of the Allies' key early objectives was the taking of Cherbourg, which had been utterly devastated by the Germans. It was critical to capture a major port intact in order to land troops, munitions and rations after the success of the initial attack. Churchill needed the port to be rebuilt so that it could act as a potential Allied supply route.

<u>Above:</u> **Churchill in Air Commodore's uniform strokes Montgomery's pet spaniel Rommel, 21st Army Group HQ, Normandy, 7 August 1944** Churchill went to Normandy to discuss with Montgomery a planned attack in the South of France. One of 'Monty's' two dogs was named after his German arch-rival, Field Marshal Erwin Rommel; the other was called Hitler.

<u>Left:</u> **Churchill with some of the troops who led the D-Day assault, near Caen, 22 July 1944** 'The nights were very noisy, there being repeated raids by single aircraft, and more numerous alarms,' Churchill wrote about his visit to the battle zone. 'By day I studied the whole process of the landing of supplies and troops, both at the piers, in which I had so long been interested, and on the beaches. On one occasion six tank landing-craft came to the beach in line. When their prows grounded their drawbridges fell forward and out came the tanks, three or four from each, and splashed ashore. In less than eight minutes by my stopwatch the tanks stood in column of route on the highroad ready to move into action. This was an impressive performance, and typical of the rate of discharge which had now been achieved. I was fascinated to see the DUKWs [amphibious trucks] swimming through the harbour, waddling ashore, and then hurrying up the hill to the great dump where the lorries were waiting to take their supplies to the various units. Upon the wonderful efficiency of this system, now yielding results far greater than we had ever planned, depended the hopes of a speedy and victorious action.'

In October 1944, Churchill engaged in nearly
two weeks' negotiation with Stalin in Moscow
concerning the post-war fate of Eastern Europe.

Opposite: **Churchill watches an
assault against enemy positions
north of Florence from a forward
observation post, August 1944**
On 26 August 1944, Churchill visited
a Royal Artillery battery near
Florence, where he signed a shell
before it was fired into the German
lines on a ridge across the valley.
He then observed the battle from a
ruined house that had been held by the
Germans only two days previously.
When British shells landed in the
target area, he remembered his
autographed shell and remarked:
'This is rather like sending a rude
letter and being there when it arrives.'

General Alexander took Churchill
to the front line. 'The Germans were
firing with rifles and machine-guns
from thick scrub on the farther side of
the valley, about five hundred yards
away,' Churchill recalled. 'Our front
line was beneath us. The firing was
desultory and intermittent. But this
was the nearest I got to the enemy
and the time I heard most bullets in
the Second World War.' Alexander
described Churchill's delight: 'There
were quite a lot of shells flying about,
and land mines all over the place. He
absolutely loved it; it fascinated him –
the real warrior at heart.'

Above: **Clementine greets Churchill on his return from Moscow, 22 October 1944**
During his negotiations with Stalin in Moscow, Churchill produced what he
called his 'naughty document'. It ranked five European countries – Romania,
Greece, Hungary, Yugoslavia and Bulgaria – according to the 'proportional
interest' of the Allied powers. Stalin studied the percentages on the list, made a
large tick on it with a blue pencil and passed it back. Churchill commented wryly:
'Might it not be thought rather cynical if it seemed we had disposed of these issues,
so fateful to millions of people, in such an off-hand manner? Let us burn the paper.'
To which Stalin replied: 'No, you keep it.'

On the morning of 22 October, Churchill flew from Naples to London, arriving
in the afternoon after a six-and-a-half-hour flight; his total flying time from
Moscow had been more than 24 hours. Met at the airport by Clementine, he was
driven to Chequers, where his daughters Sarah and Diana were among those
waiting to welcome him. His Principal Private Secretary John Martin wrote to
Randolph that 'he looks none the worse for his journeys and seems to me to have
returned from Moscow fitter and in better spirits than he has been for a long time'.

'The Big Three' at the Yalta Conference, Crimea, February 1945
The purpose of the Yalta Conference was to discuss the reorganization of post-war Europe. Roosevelt, who was already extremely ill, died two months later, on 12 April 1945.

On 9 February, at Yalta, Churchill proposed a toast to Stalin: 'I hope to see the future of Russia bright, prosperous, and happy. I will do anything to help, and I am sure so will the President ... The fire of war has burnt up the misunderstandings of the past... We feel we have a friend whom we can trust, and I hope he will continue to feel the same about us.'

Five days after Roosevelt's death, Churchill told the House of Commons: '[A]t Yalta I noticed that the President was ailing. His captivating smile, his gay and charming manner, had not deserted him, but his face had a transparency, an air of purification, and often there was a far-away look in his eyes. When I took my leave of him in Alexandria harbour I must confess that I had an indefinable sense of fear that his health and his strength were on the ebb. But nothing altered his inflexible sense of duty ... As the saying goes, he died in harness, and we may well say in battle harness, like his soldiers, sailors, and airmen, who side by side with ours are carrying on their tasks to the end all over the world. What an enviable death was his!'

Churchill said of Field Marshal Alan Brooke, Chief of the Imperial General Staff: 'When I thump the table and push my face towards him what does he do? Thumps the table harder and stares back at me.'

Left: **Churchill with Field Marshals Brooke and Montgomery on the east bank of the Rhine, 26 March 1945**
In mid-March 1945 Montgomery planned to cross the upper part of the Rhine with 80,000 Allied troops to break into the industrial Ruhr area. On 23 March, Churchill flew to Venlo, on the River Meuse in the Netherlands, to observe the action. The next day he watched the troops cross the river at several points to attack the German defences.

Brooke (later Lord Alanbrooke) was an efficient, level-headed leader and a master of strategy. In his direction of Britain's military operations, he was the ideal counterpart to Churchill, who acted on intuition and was prone to flights of fancy. The pragmatic Brooke often deflected Churchill from what he described as his 'wildest and most dangerous' schemes.

Right: **Churchill and Montgomery crossing the Rhine on a US landing craft, 25 March 1945**
On 9 March 1945, Churchill had telegraphed Eisenhower regarding his troops crossing the Rhine: 'No one who studies war can fail to be inspired by the admirable speed and flexibility of the American armies...'

On 25 March, Churchill and Montgomery crossed the Rhine themselves. 'The officers told us that the far bank was unoccupied so far as they knew,' Churchill recalled. 'So I said to Montgomery: "Why don't we go across and have a look at the other side?" Somewhat to my surprise he answered: "Why not?"...We landed in brilliant sunshine and perfect peace on the German shore, and walked about for half an hour or so unmolested.'

Churchill with the King, in his Royal Navy Uniform, the Queen, Princess Elizabeth, in her ATS uniform, and Princess Margaret, waving to the crowds outside Buckingham Palace, 'Victory in Europe Day', London, 8 May 1945

On 7 May 1945, German forces in Europe surrendered. On the following morning, Churchill worked in bed at his victory broadcast. He also sent out an enquiry to ensure there was no shortage of beer in the capital for the evening's celebrations. Shortly after one o'clock he left Downing Street for Buckingham Palace to lunch with the Royal Family and to share with them the country's triumph. The King later wrote in his diary, 'We congratulated each other on the end of the European War. The day we have been longing for has arrived at last and we can look back with thankfulness to God that our tribulation is over.' They all appeared on the palace balcony to greet a crowd of 20,000, many of whom were dressed in red, white and blue. The Royal Family came out many times to wave to the people and later, the two princesses joined the celebrations in the streets. In the evening, the palace was floodlit for the first time in six years and two searchlights made a giant 'V' above St Paul's Cathedral.

Making his way through an exhilarated crowd, Churchill crosses from the House of Commons to St Margarets Church for a Service of Thanksgiving, 8 May 1945
Returning to Downing Street, Churchill announced the unconditional surrender of Germany in a broadcast to the nation: 'Today, perhaps, we shall think mostly of ourselves ... We may allow ourselves a brief period of rejoicing; but let us not forget for a moment the toil and efforts that lie ahead. Japan, with all her treachery and greed, remains unsubdued. The injury she has inflicted on Great Britain, the United States, and other countries, and her detestable cruelties, call for justice and retribution. We must now devote all our strength and resources to the completion of our task, both at home and abroad. Advance, Britannia. Long live the cause of freedom. God save the King.' He then went to the Commons to repeat the statement, adding that 'I wish to give my hearty thanks to men of all parties, to everyone in every part of the House wherever they sit...'

Below: **Churchill and Clementine campaign in his Woodford constituency, July 1945**
Although general elections had been suspended during the war, one was called on 5 July 1945, even before the Japanese had surrendered. As it took considerable time for the votes to be received from the troops serving overseas, the result was not declared until 26 July. Churchill said of Clementine, who had been at his side throughout all the elections in which he had stood: 'My marriage was much the most fortunate and joyous event which happened to me in the whole of my life, for what can be more glorious than to be united in one's walk through life with a being incapable of an ignoble thought?'

<u>Above:</u> **Churchill addresses the crowd, London, 8 May 1945**
Churchill was given a roaring ovation when he appeared with his Cabinet colleagues on a balcony in Whitehall. 'God bless you all. This is your victory,' he said, to which the crowd shouted back: 'No – it is yours.' He continued: 'It is the victory of the cause of freedom in every land. In all our long history we have never seen a greater day than this. Everyone, man or woman, has done their best. Everyone has tried. Neither the long years, nor the dangers, nor the fierce attacks of the enemy, have in any way weakened the independent resolve of the British nation. God bless you all.' Returning to the balcony later, he said: 'A terrible foe has been cast to the ground, and awaits our judgement and our mercy.'

Churchill with Eisenhower, who was awarded the Freedom of the City of London, 12 June 1945

Eisenhower was presented with this honour as a symbol of the British people's appreciation of his leadership in their great time of need. 'Never have I seen a man so staunch in pursuing the purpose in hand, so ready to accept responsibility for misfortune, or so generous in victory,' Churchill declared of Eisenhower at Mansion House.

Addressing the Guildhall, Eisenhower said: 'Kinship among nations is not determined in such measurements as proximity, size and age. Rather we should turn to those inner things, call them what you will – I mean those intangibles that are the real treasures free men possess. To preserve his freedom of worship, his equality before the law, his liberty to speak and act as he sees fit, subject only to the provision that we trespass not upon similar rights of others – the Londoner will fight! So will the citizen of Abilene! When we consider these things then the valley of the Thames draws closer to the farms of Kansas and the plains of Texas.'

Rather than wait at home for two weeks for the results of the general election held on 5 July 1945, Churchill decided to take a fortnight's holiday in France, the first he had had since war began.

The Churchills on holiday at Hendaye, France, July 1945

Before the general election, the Conservative Central Office forecast a majority of at least a hundred seats for the government. In the meantime, the Canadian Brigadier-General Brutinel offered Churchill his house in the French Basque country and he and Clementine went on holiday. Mary Churchill recalled: 'Winston at first low and tired but the magic of painting soon laid hold of him, absorbing him for hours on end, and banishing disturbing thoughts of either the present or future.... But over us the tantalizing cloud of uncertainty: what did the ballot boxes hold?'

In the mornings the Churchills bathed from a sandy beach. Jock Colville gave a vivid description: 'The Prime Minister floated, like a benevolent hippo, in the middle of a large circle of protective French policemen who duly donned bathing suits for the purpose. His British detective had also been equipped by...Scotland Yard for such aquatic duties. Round and round this circle swam a persistent French Countess, a notorious collaborateuse who hoped by speaking to Churchill to escape the fate which the implacable Resistance were probably planning for her. It reminded me of the medieval practice of "touching for the King's evil".'

**Churchill sits on the edge of a damaged chair outside
Hitler's underground bunker, Berlin, 15 July 1945**
On 30 April 1945, Adolf Hitler took a cyanide capsule and
shot himself next to Eva Braun, whom he had married 40
hours earlier. She had also poisoned herself. The bodies
were burned by Hitler's valet and SS adjutant Otto Günsche.
Their remains were later found and buried by the Russians.

On the afternoon of 15 July, Churchill and his daughter
Mary flew from Bordeaux to Berlin to visit the ruins of
Hitler's Chancellery and the *Führerbunker*. Churchill wrote
of the experience: 'In the square in front of the Chancellery...
except for one old man who shook his head disapprovingly,
they all began to cheer. My hate had died with their
surrender.' Later he recalled: 'I went down to the bottom and
saw the room in which he and his mistress had committed
suicide, and when we came up again they showed us the
place where his body had been burned.'

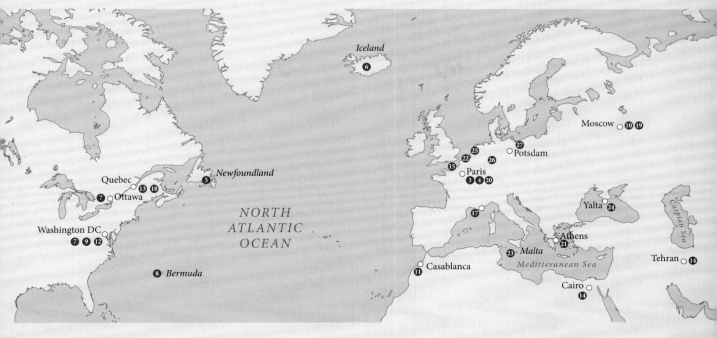

Wartime travels

During his five years as Prime Minister, Churchill made 27 overseas journeys to co-ordinate British war policy with Britain's allies, and to visit British, Commonwealth and Allied troops.

1–4. Paris, 16–17 May 1940; 30 May 1940; Briare, 11–12 June 1940, Tours, 13 June 1940
Churchill meets with French leaders
5. Newfoundland, 9–12 August 1941
Atlantic Conference: Roosevelt and Churchill issue Atlantic Charter
6. Iceland, 16 August 1941
Churchill inspects British and US troops
7. Washington, 22–28 December 1941
First Washington Conference: Roosevelt and Churchill work out details of Anglo-American co-operation
Ottawa, 29–31 December 1941
Churchill speaks to Canadian Parliament
8. Bermuda, 14–16 January 1942
Churchill visits British garrison
9. Washington, 18–22 June 1942
Second Washington Conference: Churchill urges Roosevelt to support attack on Italy, the 'soft underbelly' of the Axis
10. Moscow, 12–16 August 1942
First Moscow Conference: Churchill tells Stalin 'No Second Front' possible
11. Casablanca, 14–24 January 1943

Casablanca Conference: meeting between Roosevelt and Churchill. Unconditional surrender of Germany declared Allied aim
12. Washington, 12–25 May 1943
Third Washington Conference: Roosevelt and Churchill make decision to invade Italy after Sicily
Algiers and Tunis, 28 May – 4 June 1943
13. Quebec, 10–31 August 1943
First Quebec Conference: Churchill and Roosevelt discuss plans for Allied invasions of Italy and France
14. Cairo, 21–27 November 1943
First Cairo Conference: Churchill urges Roosevelt to give priority to the war in the Mediterranean
Tehran, 7 November – 2 December 1943
Tehran Conference: Stalin, Roosevelt and Churchill meet to discuss future strategy. Churchill promises Second Front early in 1944; confirmation of Normandy landings
Cairo, 2–11 December 1943
Second Cairo Conference: confirmation of Allied strategy against Japan
15. Normandy, 12 June 1944,
D-Day: Churchill visits Normandy beaches
16. Italy, 10–29 August 1944
Churchill visits Italian Front
17. South of France, 15 August 1944
Churchill watches US amphibious landing
18. Quebec, 11–17 September 1944
Second Quebec Conference: Churchill discusses British contribution to the war in

the Pacific with Roosevelt
19. Moscow, 9–10 October 1944
Second Moscow Conference: Churchill and Stalin discuss Poland, Bulgaria and Yugoslavia
20. Paris, 10–12 November 1944
Churchill visits liberated Paris, French Front
21. Athens, 25–28 December 1944
Churchill travels to Greece to oppose Communist takeover
22. Paris, 3–4 January 1945
Brussels, 5 January 1945
Churchill visits front line in France and Belgium
23. Malta, 30 January – 3 February 1945
Malta Conference: Churchill and Roosevelt agree on undesirability of Soviet advance in Western Europe
24. Yalta, 3–11 February 1945
Yalta Conference: Stalin, Roosevelt and Churchill discuss the defeat of Germany, the future of Poland, and the United Nations
25. Belgium and Holland, 2–6 March 1945
Churchill visits front line
26. Holland and Germany, 23–26 March 1945
Churchill visits front line and crosses the Rhine, landing in German-held territory for 30 minutes
27. Berlin, 15–27 July 1945
Potsdam Conference: Churchill, Truman and Stalin discuss post-war Europe and terms of Japan's surrender

8

The Post-War Years: 1946–1965

Churchill had led a battle-scarred Britain through the ravages of the Second World War and then lost to the Labour Party in the election. Now his doctor told him to seek out sun and tranquillity.

Churchill's doctor, Lord Moran, told him to escape the English winter and to seek out sun and tranquillity. Eight months after the end of the war, Churchill was in Florida, to experience, as he told a reporter, 'the great pleasure I feel in enjoying the genial sunshine of Miami Beach'. While there, he painted scenes of the beach and visited Hialeah Park to watch the races.

On 26 February 1946, Churchill received an honorary degree from the University of Miami. He accepted it before an audience of 17,500 at what was then known as the Burdine Stadium, later renamed the Orange Bowl. He told them that 'that no boy or girl should ever be disheartened by lack of success in their youth, but should diligently and faithfully continue to persevere and make up for lost time'. He also stressed the need for education, urging 'a generous and comprehending outlook upon the human story with all its sadness and with all its unquenchable hope'.

Wherever he went in the US, Churchill was welcomed with enthusiasm, and he received honorary degrees from a number of universities throughout the country.

Above: **Churchill and Stalin shake hands with Harry S. Truman, the new President of the US, at the Potsdam Conference, Germany, July 1945**
Potsdam was the last 'Big Three' conference that Churchill was to attend. Previously, there had always been Stalin and Roosevelt; now there was a new American President – Harry S. Truman.

With the withdrawal of the Labour Party from the wartime government, Churchill had found himself heading a Conservative caretaker administration. It was therefore necessary for the Labour leader Clement Attlee to accompany him to Potsdam, in case the election should go against the Conservatives, as it unexpectedly did. In the immediate aftermath of hostilities, the primary aim of the conference was the settlement of Europe, including the broken and defeated Germany itself.

This was the first time Churchill met Truman, who had succeeded to the presidency upon the death of Roosevelt in April. Mary Churchill wrote to her mother about their meeting: 'He told me he liked the President immensely – they talk the same language. He says he is sure he can work with him.' Churchill later wrote of Truman: 'I called on him the morning after our arrival and was impressed with his gay, precise, sparkling manner and obvious power of decision.'

Left: **Churchill's copy of** *HMS Pinafore*
It was while he was watching the 1939
film of *The Mikado* at Chequers in April
1945 that Churchill received a call
from General Alexander: the German
armies in Italy had surrendered.

'I have got tunes in my head for every
war I have been to, and indeed for
every critical or exciting phase in my
life,' he wrote. 'Some day when my ship
comes home, I am going to have them
all collected in gramophone records,
and then I will sit in a chair and smoke
my cigar, while pictures and faces,
moods and sensations long vanished
return; and pale but true there gleams
the light of other days.'

33.

From Stettin in the Baltic
    to Trieste in the Adriatic,

an iron curtain has descended
    across the Continent.

Behind that line
    lie all the capitals of the ancient states
    of Central and Eastern Europe.

Warsaw, Berlin, Prague, Vienna, Budapest,
    Belgrade, Bucharest and Sofia,

all these famous cities and the populations
                        around them

(What I must call)

lie in the Soviet sphere

and all are subject
    in one form or another,

not only to Soviet influence (in many cases)
    but to a very high and increasing
    measure of control fr Moscow.

W.S.C.

Churchill's notes for his 'Iron Curtain' speech, which he gave at Westminster College, Fulton, Missouri, 5 March 1946

From Miami Churchill went to Washington, where he had dinner with Truman at the White House. He used the opportunity to try out a speech he was due to give in Fulton, Missouri. Both Truman and Secretary of State James Byrnes 'seemed to like it very well', Churchill wrote to Attlee. Byrnes was 'excited about it and did not suggest any alterations'. Attlee in reply told him, 'I am sure your Fulton speech will do good.'

At Westminster College in Fulton, Churchill was introduced to the audience by President Truman. He gave a speech he had called 'Sinews of Peace' but it quickly became known as the 'Iron Curtain', which he said had descended across Europe. In this speech, Churchill warned of the twin dangers of war and tyranny, and argued forcefully in favour of a 'special relationship' between Britain and the United States. 'I repulse the idea that a new war is inevitable; still more that it is imminent,' he declared during the course of the speech. 'I do not believe that Soviet Russia desires war. What they desire is the fruits of war and the indefinite expansion of their power and doctrines. But what we have to consider here to-day while time remains, is the permanent prevention of war and the establishment of conditions of freedom and democracy as rapidly as possible in all countries...'

In March 1946, Churchill travelled to New York
in order to secure support for a fairer loan for
the British from the American government.

Churchill in New York, March 1946

On 15 March 1946, Churchill attended a reception at New York's Waldorf Astoria Hotel, where he spoke of 'the curse of war, and the darker curse of tyranny' but also of relations between Britain and the US. 'I have never asked for an Anglo-American military alliance or a treaty,' he told the audience. 'I asked for something different and in a sense...something more. I asked for fraternal association, free, voluntary, fraternal association... it will come to pass, as surely as the sun will rise to-morrow.' Churchill went on to say that nothing could stop the two countries 'drawing even closer to one another and nothing can obscure the fact that, in their harmonious companionship, lies the main hope of a world instrument for maintaining peace on earth and goodwill to all men'.

On 20 March, Churchill left America. He was interviewed by his son Randolph, who asked: 'Have you got any message to give the United States on your departure?' Churchill replied: 'The United States must realize its power and its virtue. It must pursue consistently the great themes and principles which have made it the land of the free. All the world is looking to the American democracy for resolute guidance. If I could sum it up in a phrase I would say, "Dread nought, America."'

In 1941, Churchill was appointed as Lord Warden
and Admiral of the Cinque Ports. In August 1946,
his investiture finally took place at Dover Castle.

**Accompanied by Clementine, Churchill is installed as Lord
Warden and Admiral of the Cinque Ports, Dover Castle,
14 August 1946**
On 24 September 1941, *The Times* reported on Churchill's
appointment as Lord Warden and Admiral of the Cinque
Ports: 'As First Lord in two wars he has fully qualified to
preside in this ancient shrine of the seafaring tradition.'
After a delay of five years, the time had now come for his
investiture. It was an impressive ceremony, and cheering

crowds lined the route from Dover Castle. Churchill
responded with his traditional V-sign. As a salute of 19
guns boomed, the church's bells pealed out as they had
done on hearing the news from Agincourt. In his speech
he declared: 'One thing at least we can promise to all: in
our own place and in our own way, this glorious and pure
foreshore of England, the shrine of its Christianity, the
cradle of its institutions, the bulwark of its defence, will
still do its best for all.'

Churchill gives his 11 year-old grandson Julian Sandys a warm embrace, 1947

Julian Sandys (1936–97) was the oldest child of Diana and Duncan Sandys. The Sandys often spent Christmas with the Churchills and on Boxing Day 1947 Clementine wrote: '[T]ook Edwina [Julian's sister] & Julian to the Big Circus at Olympia & they loved it. It was Edwina's 9th birthday. She is a very pretty little girl & may be a "Beauty" one day I think. Diana came too & we really had a delightful afternoon.'

Edwina (born 1938) went on to become a sculptor. One of her works, titled *Breakthrough* and featuring sections of the Berlin Wall, is in Fulton, Missouri, where her grandfather made his famous 'Iron Curtain' speech. Julian studied law and in 1983 became a Queen's Counsel.

Churchill feeds Digger the albino kangaroo, London Zoo, 10 September 1947

Digger the kangaroo was a present to Churchill from the Australian Stockbreeders' Association. He may well have travelled from Sydney by ship, but it is possible that he came by aeroplane: Qantas first flew the Kangaroo Route in 1947, carrying 29 passengers and 11 crew from Sydney to London via Darwin, Singapore, Kolkata, Karachi, Cairo and Tripoli – a journey time of 93 hours in total, 55 of them in the air.

A persistent theme of Churchill's speeches while he was Leader of the Opposition was the unity of Europe. In May 1948 he spoke at the Hague Congress in favour of a European Assembly.

Churchill receives applause from the leaders of the European movement – Pieter Aadrian Kerstens, Paul Ramadier, Dr Joseph Retinger (Secretary-General of the International Committee of the Movements for European Unity) and Denis de Rougemont – following his speech at the Congress of Europe, Hall of Knights, The Hague, Holland, 7 May 1948

In May 1948, Churchill gave a speech at the Congress of Europe, held at The Hague. 'President Roosevelt spoke of the Four Freedoms, but the one the matters today is Freedom from Fear,' he told the delegates. 'A high and a solemn responsibility rests upon us here. If we allow ourselves to be rent and disordered by pettiness and small disputes, if we fail in clarity of view or courage in action, a priceless occasion may be cast away for ever. But if we all pull together and pool the luck and the comradeship – and we shall need all the comradeship and not a little luck if we are to move together in this way – and firmly grasp the larger hopes of humanity, then it may be that we shall move into a happier sunlit age, when all the little children who are now growing up in this tormented world may find themselves not the victors nor the vanquished in the fleeting triumphs of one country over another in the bloody turmoil of destructive war, but the heirs of all the treasures of the past and the masters of all the science, the abundance and the glories of the future.'

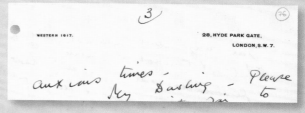

Letter from Clementine to Winston, 5 March 1949

Churchill planned to visit Max Beaverbrook in Jamaica while on his way to America. Clementine wrote to him:

> …I feel that for you, at this moment of doubt and discouragement among your followers, to stay with Max will increase that doubt & discouragement. It would seem cynical and an insult to the Party…
>
> I do not mind if you resign the Leadership when things are good, but I can't bear you to be accepted murmuringly and uneasily …now & then I have felt chilled & discouraged by the creeping knowledge that you do only just as much as will keep you in Power. But that much is not enough in these hard anxious times.

Churchill accepted his wife's advice. On 18 March, he set sail for New York, almost 55 years after his first Atlantic crossing.

On 7 April 1949, Truman finally made the statement Churchill had been urging him to make: that he would 'not hesitate' to use the atom bomb if it were necessary for the welfare of the United States or for the democracies of the world.

Churchill returns from the US on the *Queen Mary*, April 1949

In spring 1949, Churchill had been invited to speak at the Massachusetts Institute of Technology in Boston, among other venues in America. In his speech at MIT, he said: 'Little did we guess that what has been called the Century of the Common Man would witness, as its outstanding feature, more common men killing each other with greater facilities than any other five centuries put together in the history of the world.' Of the 'fundamental schism' that Communism had created with the rest of mankind, he said: 'The machinery of propaganda may pack their minds with falsehood and deny them truth for many generations of time, but the soul of man thus held in trance, or frozen in a long night, can be awakened by a spark coming from God knows where, and in a moment the whole structure of lies and oppression is on trial for its life.'

On his return to England he wrote to Truman: 'I was greatly impressed by your statement about not fearing to use the atomic bomb if the need arose. I am sure this will do more than anything else to ward off the catastrophe of a third world war.'

**Churchill meets the crowds
on the day of the general election,
23 February 1950**

On 11 January 1950, Churchill's
winter holiday in Madeira was cut
short by the announcement of the
dissolution of Parliament. As Leader
of the Opposition, he rushed back
by specially chartered flying-boat,
saying: 'I heard there was going to be
a general election, so I thought I had

better come back in case I was wanted.'
At Chartwell, he set about writing the
Conservative election manifesto.

In his first party political broadcast
of the campaign, Churchill told
listeners that the choice before them
was 'whether we should take another
plunge into Socialist regimentation, or
by a strong effort, regain the freedom,
initiative and opportunity of British
life'. On 17 February, he called for 'one

heave' of Britain's shoulders
to 'shake herself free' from the
Socialist burden.

On 16 February 1950 it was widely
reported that Churchall had died.
Commenting on the rumour of his
death, he said: 'It would have been
more artistic to keep this one for
Polling Day.'

In the 1950 General Election, Labour defeated the Conservatives again but with a majority of only five seats over all other parties. Both Churchill's sons-in-law, Duncan Sandys and Christopher Soames, were elected, but his son Randolph lost at his fourth attempt.

Above: **Churchill leaves the Wanstead Conservative Club with a bulldog called Token, Woodford, 23 February 1950**
After the election Churchill remained Leader of the Opposition, yet moves were afoot to replace him with someone younger, in particular Anthony Eden. Another hopeful, Anthony Barber, wrote to Churchill: 'To most of the young candidates like myself it was a great inspiration to have a man of your personality and experience at the helm ... your leadership since the end of the war has been one of the most vital factors which has brought our Party back to its present position.' However, Churchill made it to the next general election, which took place on 25 October 1951.

Opposite: **Churchill and a four-month-old thoroughbred filly, Chartwell, 1950**
By the end of 1948, Churchill had given up riding, but in 1949 he found a new passion – racehorses. He registered in his father's colours and bought a grey French colt, Colonist II, which won 13 races and large sums in prize money, before being sold to stud in 1951. In 1950, Churchill was made a member of the Jockey Club. In 1955, he acquired a small stud farm at Newchapel Green, Lingfield (near Chartwell), where he bred some fine horses and enjoyed considerable success.

While Churchill was in Brighton for the Conservative Party Conference in October 1947, his poodle Rufus was run over. Later, introducing his new dog, Churchill would say: 'His name is Rufus II, but the II is silent.'

Below: Churchill with his miniature russet poodle Rufus II, Chartwell, 23 February 1950
Churchill was given Rufus II by Walter Graebner, his *Life* magazine editor for his war memoirs.

Opposite: Notes for Churchill's speech on receiving a PhD from Copenhagen University, 11 October 1950
In his speech, Churchill emphasized that 'the first duty of a university is to teach wisdom, not a trade; character, not technicalities'.

Your Majesties, Your Royal Highnesses,
    Your Excellencies,
        Mr. Rector,
            Professors, Ladies and Gentlemen:

I am very proud and very grateful
    to receive a Degree of Philosophy
        fm the famous University of Copenhagen.

As life unfolds I hv bn astonished to find
    how many more degrees I hv received
        than I hv passed examinations.

I was never very good at those,

But now I am treated as if I were
    quite a learned man.

This is a good argument for not being
    discouraged by the failures
        or shortcomings of youth,

    but to persevere
        and go on trying to learn all your life.

=

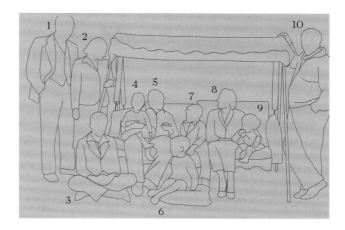

Winston Churchill surrounded by members of his family on The Pink Terrace, Chartwell, September 1951

Key to the photograph:
1) Duncan Sandys 2) Diana Sandys 3) Julian Sandys
4) Emma Soames 5) Winston Churchill 6) Nicholas Soames
7) Winston Churchill Jr 8) Clementine Churchill
9) Arabella Churchill 10) Randolph Churchill

In 1947, Mary Churchill had married Christopher Soames, a Guards Officer whom she met when he was Assistant Military Attaché in Paris. Soames would become a good companion to Winston in the running of Chartwell Farm, as well as encouraging him in his horse-racing.

Clementine described little Winston Jr, Randolph's son with his first wife, Pamela, as 'charming with his Mama'. In 1948 Randolph married June Osborne and a year later their only child together, Arabella, was born. A month later, the political lives of both Winston Churchill's son and his son-in-law were to change. In the 1950 General Election Randolph was yet again unsuccessful at his attempt to get in to Parliament; he never stood again. Duncan Sandys fared better, but not as well as originally planned. Clementine wrote to her husband of her son-in-law's position in government: 'Do not be angry with me – But first do you not think it would be wiser to give Duncan a smaller post – Secretary of State for War is so very prominent – then do you think it wise to have him working immediately under your orders as Minister of Defence [Churchill's combined office with that of Prime Minister until 1952]. If anything were to go wrong it would be delicate & tricky – first of all having to defend your son-in-law, & later if by chance he made a mistake having to dismiss him...' On 31 October 1951 Duncan became Minister of Supply.

The general election of October 1951 marked the 16th time Churchill had gone to hustings since 1889.

Winston with Clementine, general election day, 26 October 1951

As the election campaign gathered intensity, the *Daily Mirror* wrote: 'Whose finger do they want on the trigger? Attlee's or Churchill's?' This idea concerned Churchill and he said at Woodford on 6 October: 'I am sure we do not want any fingers upon any trigger. Least of all do we want a fumbling finger... It may be a Russian finger, or an American finger,

or a United Nations Organization finger, but it cannot be a British finger.'

On 8 October, in his first party political broadcast of the campaign, Churchill stated that the difference between the Conservative and Socialist outlooks was like that between a ladder and a queue: 'We are all for the ladder. Let all try their best to climb. They are for the queue. Let each wait his place until his turn comes.'

Winston and Clementine make their way through the crowds outside Conservative Party HQ, Abbey House, London, 26 October 1951

Three days before the election, Churchill told an audience at Plymouth that if he remained in public life he would strive to make 'an important contribution to the prevention of a third world war, and to bringing the peace that every land fervently desired'. He dearly hoped that he might have this opportunity, declaring, 'It is the last prize I seek to win.'

Although Labour actually had more votes cast for them, the Conservatives won 321 seats against Labour's 295. When Attlee tendered his resignation, the King asked Churchill to form a new government – he was Prime Minster for a second time. Harold Macmillan was later to recall, 'It was fun to join in again, in the old scenes which reminded one of the wartime Churchill. Children, friends, ministers, private secretaries, typists all in a great flurry but all thoroughly enjoying the return to the centre of the stage.'

On 4 November, Clementine wrote to a friend: 'I do hope Winston will be able to help the country... It will be up-hill work, but he has a willing, eager heart.'

<u>Opposite:</u> **Churchill with Clementine on his 77th birthday, 30 November 1951**
Two days before his birthday, Churchill told the House of Commons that he and his Foreign Minister, Anthony Eden, held to the idea 'of a supreme effort to bridge the gulf between the two worlds, so that each of us can live its life, if not in friendship, at least without the fear, the hatreds, and the frightful waste of the "cold war"'.

His private secretary David Hunt recalled that, following a day of celebrations, Churchill 'came down to the Cabinet Room to work just the same, and with his usual thoughtfulness invited me to have a drink with him and said: "You've never seen a Prime Minister of 77 before." I replied: "No, but you have."' The last Prime Minister to have been in office at Churchill's age was Gladstone.

<u>Below:</u> **Churchill and Truman in the Oval Office, Washington DC, 5 January 1952**
Having reached New York on the *Queen Mary*, Churchill flew to Washington DC. That evening he and President Truman dined together on the presidential yacht. Fully aware of the cost of the American effort in the Korean War and of their programme of rearmament, Churchill said: 'Now the free world is not a naked world, but a rearming world.' A few days later he went to the Walter Reed Army Medical Center in Washington, where he shook hands with soldiers who had been wounded in Korea. At a dinner given by the English-Speaking Union, Churchill spoke of an unwritten alliance between the two countries: 'It is an alliance far closer in fact than many that exists in writing.'

In the early hours of 6 February 1952, King George VI died in his sleep at Sandringham. The following day, Churchill made a broadcast in which he spoke movingly of the King's illness and final days.

Churchill leaves St James's Palace after a Privy Council meeting, having been summoned to the Accession Council on the death of the Sovereign, 6 February 1952
In his broadcast, Churchill spoke of the King's last days, saying that he 'walked with death, as if death were a companion, an acquaintance whom he recognized and did not fear. In the end death came as a friend; and after a happy day of sunshine and sport, and after "good night" to those who loved him best, he fell asleep as every man or woman who strives to fear God and nothing else in the world may hope to do.' The King's funeral took place at St George's Chapel, Windsor Castle, on 15 February 1952.

From left to right, Frederick Marquis, 1st Earl of Woolton,
Anthony Eden, Clement Attlee and Churchill wait to greet
the Queen on her return from Kenya, 8 February 1952
A heavy smoker, King George VI had been unwell for some years
and had a lung removed in the summer of 1951. He made a good
enough recovery to allow Princess Elizabeth and the Duke of
Edinburgh to set off on their Commonwealth tour at the end of
January 1952; black clothes were packed, however. In Kenya,
the Princess watched the sun rise at Treetops game lodge with
the Duke's private secretary. An eagle hovered above, almost
diving down. The secretary recalled: 'I never thought about it
until later, but that was roughly the time when the King died.'

Churchill said of the newly crowned Queen Elizabeth II: 'I, whose youth was passed in the august, unchallenged and tranquil glories of the Victorian Era, may well feel a thrill in invoking, once more, the prayer and the Anthem: *God Save the Queen*'.

Churchill toasts the Queen at a banquet given to her by all Parliaments of the Commonwealth six days before her coronation, Westminster Hall, London, 27 May 1953
Queen Elizabeth II was to be crowned on 2 June 1953. In the House of Commons, Churchill spoke graciously to a crowded Chamber of the new monarch: 'A fair and youthful figure, Princess, wife and mother is the heir to all our traditions and glories never greater than in her father's days, and to all our perplexities and dangers never greater in peacetime than now. She is also heir to all our united strength and loyalty... Let us hope and pray that the accession to our ancient Throne of Queen Elizabeth the Second may be the signal for such a brightening salvation of the human scene.'

Churchill, wearing his Lord Warden uniform and Order of the Garter collar and badge, prepares to leave Buckingham Palace in a horse-drawn carriage for the coronation at Westminster Abbey, 2 June 1953

In the early part of 1953, Churchill had accepted the Queen's request that he become a Knight of the Garter. High-level meetings were being arranged following the death of Stalin in March, but all was put aside to prepare for the coronation of Queen Elizabeth II. Waving to the vast crowds, many of whom had been waiting for days to get the best view, Churchill was driven with Clementine to Westminster Abbey in a closed two-horse carriage. After the ceremony, with a mounted escort from his old regiment, the 4th Hussars, he left the procession heading for the palace and turned into Downing Street.

On the evening of 23 June 1953, Churchill suffered a stroke. Three days later, his left side was partially paralysed and he had lost the use of his left arm.

Churchill and Clementine leave St Paul's Cathedral after a Thanksgiving Service for the Coronation, 9 June 1953
At St Paul's, the Churchills had heard the young Queen's response to the Loyal and Dutiful Address, presented by representatives of the children of Christ's Hospital, founded in 1553:

'It is with great pleasure that I receive your loyal greetings in the year when you are celebrating the four-hundredth anniversary of your foundation. By its work through the years your ancient House has won a high reputation, and as your Patron I share with you your happiness on this notable landmark in its history. I am confident that your fine traditions will continue to inspire all who pass through your schools to give of their best in honourable and devoted endeavour and service, as their predecessors have in the past. May God bless the work of the schools throughout the years that lie ahead.'

Two weeks later, Churchill suffered a stroke after dinner. On the following morning, much to the astonishment of his friends and family, he insisted on presiding at a Cabinet meeting. Harold Macmillan said: 'I certainly noticed nothing beyond the fact that he was very white. He spoke little, but quite distinctly...' On 26 June, a press release announced that Churchill was in need of 'complete rest', but gave no indication as the reasons why. Churchill joked that news of his illness had stolen the limelight from the trial of serial killer John Christie.

Churchill watches the first Trooping the Colour since the Queen's coronation, 11 June 1953

As the Trooping the Colour ceremony was held in the same month as the coronation, there were larger than normal crowds in The Mall and close to Buckingham Palace. The Mall was looking impressive, with the coronation decorations still in place. Queen Elizabeth II rode side-saddle to the ceremony from Buckingham Palace, mounted on her favourite horse, Winston, and circled the Victoria Memorial outside the palace so that the crowds could see her. Following behind was Prince Philip, on a horse that seemed to have an independent spirit and was unhappy about being asked to perform in the ceremony – it went sideways and even tried to turn around. But the Prince, a skilled horseman, eventually controlled it and the horse was little calmer when he arrived at Horse Guards Parade.

When the ceremony was over, the Queen and the Guards, led by the 1st Battalion Grenadier Guards, whose colour was trooped, the Household Cavalry and the Massed Bands of the Brigade of Guards, came back up The Mall; the Queen then rode round the memorial back into the palace.

Later she came out on the balcony with the rest of the Royal Family to greet the crowds gathered outside, which had by now grown considerably.

Roger Bannister is presented to Churchill, along with his pacemakers, Chris Brasher and Chris Chataway, outside Downing Street, 1 June 1954

On 6 May 1954, medical student Roger Bannister became the first man to run the mile in under four minutes. 'I felt the tape was receding over the last few yards. I knew I could not run any faster and I gave it everything,' Bannister said of his achievement. He described the laps unfolding 'almost like the evolving of a Greek tragedy, or a triumph, in which everything is encapsulated in that short period of time'. One of the reasons why this four-minute mile record still resonates is that Bannister and his two pacemakers were amateurs. Bannister was to say later: 'It seemed to be an emergence of some new kind of desire to excel and try to tackle physical barriers. We did have something which is not so fashionable now, a kind of patriotism.'

Churchill with the Queen, Prince Charles and Princess Anne, Waterloo Station, London, 24 November 1954

As Churchill's 80th birthday approached, he was showered with presents and messages. Thousands of people both in Britain and overseas contributed £295,000 to an Eightieth Birthday Presentation Fund. Churchill put the money into a trust, the largest portion of which went towards the founding of Churchill College, Cambridge. On 30 November, members of both Houses of Parliament assembled in Westminster Hall, where he was presented with his portrait painted by Graham Sutherland. That evening, with his family around him, he celebrated at No. 10.

On 8 March 1955, Churchill confirmed to
Sir Anthony Eden that he would resign as Prime
Minister and First Lord of the Treasury on 5 April.

A man kneels in prayer outside
10 Downing St at the time of
Churchill's resignation as Prime
Minister, effective on 6 April 1955
Churchill's daughter Mary recalled
of her father's resignation: 'All of us
who were close to him understood
so well that he should be low and sad
as the day drew near. Although my
mother was intensely relieved that the
decision had been finally taken, she
knew what this moment must mean
for Winston. In my diary on 19 March
I recorded her comment to me: "It's
the first death – and for him, a death
in life."'

On 31 March 1955, Churchill wrote
to Clementine: 'I do not want to be in
London on Thursday or Friday, nor to
leave for London Airport via Downing
Street, I shall be much pestered by
people wishing to say goodbye, and
I shall be asked to go to the House of
Commons... Whereas I simply propose
to disappear and remain in strict
privacy at Chartwell till I board the
airplane for Sicily.'

On leaving 10 Downing Street
and arriving back in Chartwell, he
commented to a reporter: 'It is always
nice to come home.'

Churchill and Clementine on their Golden Wedding anniversary, with Randolph and his daughter Arabella, Villa Capponcina, Lord Beaverbrook's house at Cap d'Ail in the South of France, 12 September 1958

Tender notes between the couple show the constancy of their love. Winston wrote to Clementine: 'You have all my fondest love, my dearest. The closing days or years of life are grey and dull, but I am lucky to have you at my side. I send you my best love & many kisses. Always your devoted, W.'

Clementine replied: 'Do not be sad, my Dear One. I hope your sunshine will return. Here it is fine though of course not so warm as with you...The days are flying & soon I hope to see you safe & sound. Your loving, Clemmie.'

Churchill returns to Harrow as an Old Boy for the annual sing-song, 27 November 1958

In 1942, Churchill had praised the tradition of singing at Harrow School: 'I think the songs are very important. I know many of them by heart. I was telling the Head Master just now that I could pass an examination in some of them. They are a great treasure and possession of Harrow School, and keep the flame burning in a marvellous manner... more than could be put into bricks and mortar, or treasured in any trophies of silver or gold.'

After working for the WAAF until 1945, Churchill's daughter Sarah returned to her first great love: the theatre. In 1958, she played Peter Pan in London.

Churchill and family after watching Sarah in *Peter Pan*, Scala Theatre, London, 30 December 1958

In 1949, Sarah Churchill made her first appearance on the American stage as Tracy Lord in *The Philadelphia Story*. That year she married the photographer Anthony Beauchamp. She also appeared in *Gramercy Ghost* on Broadway and toured Britain as Eliza in *Pygmalion*.

The London newspaper *Star-News* wrote in 1958: '[Sarah] announced she will play the part in the annual Christmas production at the Scala Theatre, not one of London's plushiest but the traditional place for *Peter Pan*. Miss Churchill has been appearing sporadically on the stage and in television in America for the past nine years... Peter Pan at her age is not unusual. Mary Martin first played the part at 41 in the United States and was a big hit. Like Miss Martin and all other Peters, Miss Churchill will wear tights and fly about the stage suspended from a wire.'

Churchill attends the christening of Rupert Soames, his tenth grandchild and the fifth child of Christopher and Mary Soames, at the Wren Chapel of the Royal Hospital, Chelsea, 20 July 1959

In October 1955 Clementine had written to Churchill about their daughter Mary's husband that 'Christopher is thrilled, because Anthony [Eden] accosted him in the Members' Lobby & let him understand...that the future was rosy'. Indeed in December that year, Soames was appointed Under-Secretary of State for Air. By 1959, he had become MP for Bedford, which remained his constituency until 1966. He was made Under-Secretary of State for Air in December 1955 and Secretary of State for War in 1958. In 1965, he was briefly Shadow Foreign Secretary and in 1979 he became the last Governor of Southern Rhodesia. Christopher and Mary's son Rupert became a successful businessman.

Mary compared her relationship with her children with her mother's: '[A]fter I was married and had three or four children, we'd had a hilarious afternoon together, and afterwards, when the children went off, she said a very sad thing to me: "I see you having such fun with your children and I missed out on that with all of mine." I felt so sorry for her.'

In 1959, Churchill and Maria Callas met on Aristotle Onassis's yacht. 'It's a pleasure to travel with Sir Winston,' Callas later remarked. 'He removes from me some of the burden of my popularity.'

Churchill with Maria Callas on the *Christina O*, Monte Carlo, August 1959
Greek shipping magnate Aristotle Onassis was well known for the celebrity parties held on his yacht, which was named after his daughter. In 1959, despite his wife also being aboard, Onassis was in the midst of an affair with Maria Callas, the soprano. By the end of the cruise, both their marriages would be over.

Churchill's grand-daughter Celia Sandys, who was also on board, described Callas as 'terribly irritating' and recalls going to the Greek amphitheatre at Epidaurus, where the locals had erected a huge floral Victory-V in honour of Churchill. Callas was confused and then outraged when she realized the flowers were not for her.

Churchill and Eisenhower at the residence of US Ambassador John Hay Whitney, London, 1 September 1959
After Churchill had suffered another small stroke in April 1959, Anthony Montague Browne, his private secretary, said he was 'determined to visit America again, so that is that!' Churchill returned to the United States as the personal guest of President Eisenhower, crossing the Atlantic by jet plane for the first time. He achieved another first when he flew with the President by helicopter to his Gettysburg farm.

In September, Churchill and Eisenhower were reunited in London at a dinner marking the 20th anniversary of the outbreak of the Second World War.

Mary Churchill said of her father's last two years that 'the pace of life for Winston was very slow: it was like a broad, weary river, gently meandering on'.

In a photograph taken by Terry O'Neill, Churchill is seen being carried to an ambulance in a chair after being discharged from Middlesex Hospital, London, 21 August 1962

In June 1962, while Churchill was staying in Monte Carlo, he took a fall and broke his hip. A bed was made ready for him in a French hospital but he told his private secretary Montague Browne: 'I want to die in England.' On hearing this, Prime Minister Harold Macmillan immediately sent an RAF Comet to fly him back to London.

Carried from the plane on a stretcher, Churchill was still able to give waiting onlookers his V-sign. He was taken to the Middlesex Hospital, where he remained for six weeks. His health was still a matter of touching concern to the general public, and even minor illnesses were reported, sparking off letters of worry and good wishes. Churchill slowly recovered from the accident but his mobility was greatly impaired.

Terry O'Neill, by comparison, was a young photographer at the start of his career. In the 1960s he became internationally known, especially for his photographs of celebrities such as the Rolling Stones and the Beatles. After photographing Churchill in 1962, he went on to take pictures of the Royal Family as well as other famous politicians.

Churchill with Anthony Montague Browne, his last private secretary, and Edmund Murray, his personal detective (obscured), with deer in Richmond Park, London, 25 March 1963

Anthony Montague Browne first came to work for Winston Churchill in October 1952. A former RAF pilot, in 1945 he had been awarded the Distinguished Flying Cross. When he arrived at No. 10 for his first day of work, Churchill was on holiday with the Queen at Balmoral. Montague Browne later recalled: 'Nobody was expecting me. My first introduction to life there was being telephoned in the early hours of the morning to be told by an Admiral that our first nuclear bomb experiment had been a success. He suggested that I should wake the Prime Minister...and inform him, but even at this early stage I concluded that this would be imprudent.'

As Churchill's private secretary, Montague Browne also travelled with him. On one occasion, he witnessed a fascinating exchange in a Monte Carlo casino. Churchill was sitting at a table when Frank Sinatra passed by. Sinatra paused and, on seeing Churchill, firmly shook his hand. On leaving he was heard to say: 'I've been waiting to do that for ages.' As Montague Browne remembers, Churchill turned to him and asked: 'Who the hell was that?'

On 30 November 1964, Churchill celebrated his 90th birthday. From the window of his house at Hyde Park Gate, he acknowledged the cheers of the crowd, especially when he raised his hand in a V-sign.

DRAFT

It is very sad for me to have to end my racing activities owing to the fact that my health does not allow me to attend race meetings any more ~~or, indeed, to see anything of the horses~~.

I know that this decision will cause sorrow to you too, since we have had such a long association. My mind goes back to the Spring of 1949, when Christopher persuaded me to buy COLONIST. He gave us all great excitement and pleasure, and he was also the forerunner of many successes. I am so grateful to you for the skilful ~~and successful~~ way in which you have trained the horses that I have sent to you from my Stud. It doesn't fall to many people to start/racing career at the age of seventy-five and to reap from it such pleasure ~~and success~~.

I am so grateful to you for all that you have done, ~~and I send you~~ ~~this gift with my thanks and all good wishes.~~

Draft of a letter Churchill sent to Walter Nightingall, the trainer of his racehorses, on 27 October 1964
By the end of 1964, Churchill's health had deteriorated. It was a great blow to him when he had to give up his racehorses. His last letter to his trainer, a draft of which is shown here, makes clear his attachment to a sport that had given him such pleasure in his old age.

A decade before, Clementine had not approved of her husband's new-found enthusiasm for racing, writing to a friend in 1951: 'I do think this is a queer new facet in Winston's variegated life... Before he bought the horse (I can't think why) he had hardly been on a racecourse in his life. I must say I don't find it madly amusing.' However, she enjoyed his successes. In 1957 he remarked: 'What fun it was winning two races in one day! Quite an event for a beginner.'

Churchill's doctor Lord Moran addresses the press on the steps outside Churchill's home, 28 Hyde Park Gate, London, 18 January 1965

On 15 January 1965, Churchill suffered a stroke and on the morning of 24 January, he passed away. At his side were Lady Churchill and his children Randolph, Sarah and Mary.

His doctor and long-time associate, Lord Moran, arrived at the Hyde Park Gate townhouse at 8.35am. After the Queen and Prime Minister Harold Wilson had been informed of Churchill's death, Lord Moran's announcement was read to the assembled press outside. A spokesman said that 'Sir Winston died in peace and without pain'.

The Queen sent a message to Lady Churchill: 'The whole world is the poorer by the loss of his many-sided genius while the survival of this country and the sister nations of the Commonwealth, in the face of the greatest danger that has ever threatened them, will be a perpetual memorial to his leadership, his vision, and his indomitable courage.'

The lights of Piccadilly Circus were shut down as a sign of respect. *The Times* carried the news of Churchill's death on the front page, where in those days it would normally have run classified advertisements, and described him as 'The Greatest Englishman of his Time'.

Churchill's coffin is carried down the steps of St Paul's Cathedral by eight guardsmen after the funeral service, London, 30 January 1965

Churchill's state funeral was only the seventh given to a commoner in the last hundred years. As they were carrying the heavy coffin up the steps of St Paul's Cathedral, the bearer party had to come to a difficult halt when the 82-year-old Clement Attlee, who had succeeded Churchill as Prime Minister in 1945, stumbled in front of them. The funeral service was attended by many heads of state. It concluded poignantly with the sounding of the *Last Post* and *Reveille* by a trumpeter high up in the Whispering Gallery.

Mary Churchill had written to her father six months before his death: 'In addition to the feelings a daughter has for a loving generous father, I owe you what every Englishman, woman and child does – Liberty itself.'

'He had sympathy, incredibly wide sympathy, for ordinary people all over the world,' wrote Attlee, Churchill's wartime deputy and a lifelong Socialist, adding: 'We have lost the greatest Englishman of our time – I think the greatest citizen of the world of our time.'

By decree of the Queen, Churchill's body lay in state in Westminster Hall for three days. The nation mourned, showing its respect and its grief as 300,000 people filed past his coffin.

Members of the public watch the funeral procession from a bomb site on Ludgate Hill, London, 30 January 1965
Churchill's funeral procession was watched by thousands of people in the streets of London and by millions more on television. Men and women wept as the coffin was borne past them on a gun-carriage.

The draped coffin was then taken by launch along the Thames to Waterloo Station, and on by train to the parish church at Bladon in Oxfordshire.

Churchill's funeral launch on the Thames, London, 30 January 1965
Flying low above the Thames, four Royal Air Force Lightings passed over the Port of London launch *Havengore* (the third launch from front) carrying Churchill's coffin to Waterloo Station. The dockyard cranes, seen on the right, were dipped in his honour for the occasion.

'His body will be carried on the Thames, a river full of history. With one heart we all feel, with one mind we all acknowledge, that it will never have borne a more precious burden, or been enriched by more splendid memories.'

Sir Robert Menzies, the Prime Minister of Australia, addressing the congregation in St Paul's in the final part of his tribute to Churchill

Churchill's coffin in Bladon churchyard, Oxfordshire, 30 January 1965
It was Churchill's wish that he be buried at Bladon, next to his parents and his brother Jack and within sight of his birthplace, Blenheim Palace.

'The span of mortals is short, the end universal; and the tinge of melancholy which accompanies decline and retirement is in itself an anodyne,' Churchill wrote in his book on Marlborough. 'It is foolish to waste lamentations upon the closing phase of human life. Noble spirits yield themselves willingly to the successively falling shades which carry them to a better world or to oblivion.'

We meet to honor a man whose honor requires no meeting – for he is the most honored and honorable man to walk the stage of human history in the time in which we live.

Whenever and wherever tyranny threatened, he has always championed liberty.

Facing firmly toward the future, he has never forgotten the past.

Serving six monarchs of his native Great Britain, he has served all men's freedom and dignity.

In the dark days and darker nights when Britain stood alone – and most men save Englishmen despaired of England's life – he mobilized the English language and sent it into battle. The incandescent quality of his words illuminated the courage of his countrymen.

Given unlimited powers by his citizens, he was ever vigilant to protect their rights.

Indifferent himself to danger, he wept over the sorrows of others.

A child of the House of Commons, he became in time its father.

Accustomed to the hardships of battle, he has no distaste for pleasure.

Now his stately Ship of Life, having weathered the severest storms of a troubled century, is anchored in tranquil waters, proof that courage and faith and the zest for freedom are truly indestructible. The record of his triumphant passage will inspire free hearts for all time.

By adding his name to our rolls, we mean to honor him – but his acceptance honors us far more. For no statement or proclamation can enrich his name – the name Sir Winston Churchill is already legend.

Remarks made by President John F. Kennedy at the White House, Washington DC, on bestowing honorary US citizenship on Sir Winston Churchill, 9 April 1963

Bibliography

BOOKS

Arthur, Max, *Lost Voices of the Royal Navy*, London: Hodder & Stoughton, 2005

Arthur, Max, *Forgotten Voices of the Great War*, London: Ebury, 2002

Birkenhead, Frederick Winston Furneaux Smith, Earl, *Churchill 1874–1922*, London: Harrap, 1989

Bonham Carter, Violet, *Winston Churchill As I Knew Him*, London: Weidenfeld & Nicholson, 1955

Chaplin, E. D. W. (ed.), *Winston Churchill and Harrow: Memories of the Prime Minister's Schooldays, 1888–1892*, Harrow: Harrow School Bookshop, 1941

Churchill, Randolph S., *Winston Churchill, Volume I, Youth 1874–1900*, London: Heinemann, 1966

Churchill, Randolph S., *Winston Churchill, Volume II, Young Statesman 1901–1914*, London: Heinemann, 1966

Churchill, Randolph S. & Helmut Gernsheim (eds.), *Churchill: His Life in Photographs*, London: The Reprint Society, 1956

Churchill, Winston S., *The River War*, London: Longmans Green, 1899

Churchill, Winston S., *The Grand Alliance: The Second World War, Volume III* (1948), New York: Rosetta Books, 2010

Churchill, Winston S., *Triumph and Tragedy: The Second World War, Volume VI* (1953), London: Penguin Classics, 2005

Churchill, Winston S., *Secret Session Speeches*, London: Cassell & Co Ltd, 1946

Churchill, Winston S., *Great Contemporaries*, London: Cooper, 1990

Churchill, Winston S., *Maxims & Reflections*, New York: Barnes & Noble, 1992

Churchill, Winston S., *My Early Life: A Roving Commission* (1930), London: The Reprint Society, 1944

Churchill, Winston S., *The Collected Essays of Sir Winston Churchill, Vol. IV, Churchill at Large*, London: Library of Imperial History, 1975

Churchill, Winston S., *Thoughts and Adventures* (1932), London: Mandarin, 1990

Churchill, Winston S., *Lord Randolph Churchill*, London: Macmillan, 1906

Churchill, Winston S., *Marlborough: His Life and Times, Book Two*, Chicago: University of Chicago Press, 2002

Churchill, Winston S., *The World Crisis, Volumes I–VI*, London: Thornton Butterworth Limited, 1923-1931

Colville, John, *The Churchillians*, London: Weidenfeld and Nicolson, c.1981

Coughlin, Con, *Churchill's First War: Young Winston and the Fight Against the Taliban*, London: Pan Books, 2014

Cowles, Virginia, *Winston Churchill: The Era and the Man*, London: Hamish Hamilton, 1953

Ellis, Jennifer, *Royal Mother: The Story of Queen Mother Elizabeth and Her Family*, London: Hutchinson, 1953

Fields, Alonzo, *My 21 Years in The White House*, New York: Coward-McCann, 1961

Gilbert, Martin, *Winston S. Churchill, Volume III: The Challenge of War, 1914–1916* (1971), London: Minerva, 1990

Gilbert, Martin, *Winston S. Churchill, Volume IV: World in Torment, 1916–1922*, London: Heinemann, 1975

Gilbert, Martin, *Winston S. Churchill, Volume V: The Prophet of Truth, 1922–1939*, London: Heinemann, 1979

Gilbert, Martin, *Winston S. Churchill, Volume VI: Finest Hour, 1939–1941*, London: Heinemann, 1983

Gilbert, Martin, *Winston S. Churchill, Volume VII: Road to Victory, 1941–1945*, London: Heinemann, 1986

Gilbert, Martin, *Winston S. Churchill, Volume VIII: Never Despair, 1945–1965*, London: Heinemann, 1988

Gilbert, Martin, *Churchill and America*, London: The Free Press, 2005

Gilbert, Martin, *Churchill at War: 1941–1945, His Finest Hour in Photographs*, London: Carlton Books Limited, 2003

Gilbert, Martin, *Churchill: A Photographic Portrait*, New Jersey: Wing Books, 1993 edition

Gilbert, Martin, *The Churchill War Papers, Volume II, Never Surrender*, London: Heinemann, 1994

Gilbert, Martin, *The Churchill War Papers, Volume III, The Ever-Widening War*, London: Heinemann, 2000

Gilbert, Martin, *Churchill: A Biography*, London: Park Lane Press, 1979

Gilbert, Martin, *Churchill: A Life*, London: Heinemann, 1992

Gilbert, Martin, *Winston Churchill: The Wilderness Years*, London: Macmillan, 1981

Gilbert, Martin, *Finest Hour: Winston S. Churchill, 1939–41*, London: Heinemann, 1989

Gilbert, Martin, *Churchill's Political Philosophy*, Oxford: Oxford University Press, 1981

Gilbert, Martin (ed.), *The Power of Words*, London: Bantam Press, 2012

Grey, Viscount of Fallodon, *Twenty-Five Years, 1892–1916*, New York: Frederick A. Stokes, 1925

Halle, Kay, *Irrepressible Churchill: A Treasury of Winston Churchill's Wit*, New York: World Publishing Company, 1966

Hickman, Tom, *Churchill's Bodyguard*, London: Headline Book Publishing, 2006 edition

Howard, Jean E. and Marion F. O'Connor, *Shakespeare Reproduced: The Text in History and Ideology*, London: Methuen, 1987

Isaacson, Walter, *Einstein: His Life and Universe*, London: Simon & Schuster, 2007

Langworth, Richard M. (ed.), *Churchill by Himself: The Life, Times, Opinions of Winston Churchill in his Own Words*, St Ives: Ebury Press, 2008

Lee, Celia & John, *The Churchills: A Family Portrait*, Basingstoke: Palgrave Macmillan, 2010

Manchester, William, *The Last Lion: Winston Spencer Churchill*, Boston: Little, Brown, 1983–1988

Marsh, Edward Howard, Sir, *A Number of People, A Book of Reminiscences*, London: Harper & Brother, 1939

McGinty, Stephen, *Churchill's Cigar*, London: Pan Macmillan, 2007

Moorehead, A., *Churchill: A Pictorial Biography*, London: Panther, 1964 edition

Morin, Relman, *Churchill: Portrait of Greatness*, Englewood Cliffs: Prentice-Hall, 1965

Murray, Edmund, *I Was Churchill's Bodyguard*, London: W. H. Allen, 1987

Navaksy, Victor S., *The Art of Controversy: Political Cartoons and Their Enduring Power*, New York: Knopf Doubleday, 2013

Paterson, Michael, *Winston Churchill: The Photobiography*, Cincinnati: David & Charles, 2006

Paterson, Michael, *Winston Churchill: Personal Accounts of the Great Leader at War, 1895–1945*, Ohio: David & Charles, 2006

Pawle, Gerald, *The War and Colonel Warden*, London: Transworld Publishers, 1965

Perkin, Harold, *The Rise of Professional Society: England Since 1880*, London: Routledge, 1989

Peterson, Christian A., *Edward Steichen: The Portraits*, Minneapolis Institute of Arts: Art Museum Association of America, 1984

Russell, Douglas S., *Winston Churchill: Soldier*, London: Conway, 2006

Sandys, Celia, *From Winston With Love and Kisses: The Young Churchill*, London: Sinclair-Stevenson, 1994

Scott, George Edwin, *Rise and Fall of the League of Nations*, London: Hutchinson, 1973

Shelden, Michael, *Young Titan: The Making of Winston Churchill*, London: Simon & Schuster, 2014 edition

Singer, Barry, *Churchill Style: The Art of Being Winston Churchill*, New York: Abrams Image, 2012

Soames, Mary, *Family Album: A Personal Selection from Four Generations of Churchills*, Boston: Houghton Mifflin Company, 1982

Soames, Mary (ed.), *Speaking for Themselves: The Personal Letters of Winston and Clementine Churchill*, London: Black Swan Books, 1999

Soames, Mary, *Clementine Churchill: The Biography of a Marriage*, London: Mariner Books, 2003

Stelzer, Cita, *Dinner with Churchill: Policy-Making at the Dinner Table*, London: Short Books, 2012 edition

Stevenson, Frances, edited by A. J. P. Taylor, *Lloyd George: A Diary*, London: Hutchinson & Co., 1971

Storr, Anthony, *Churchill's Black Dog and Other Phenomena of the Human Mind*, New York: Grove Press, 1988

Taylor, Robert Lewis, *Winston Churchill: An Informal Study of Greatness*, Garden City, New York: Doubleday, 1952

Thompson, Walter, *Assignment: Churchill*, London: Popular Library, 1955

Vanderbilt Balsan, Consuelo, *The Glitter and the Gold* (1952), London: St Martin's Press, 2012

Various, edited by A. W. Lawrence,
T. E. Lawrence by his Friends, London:
J. Cape, 1954

Williamson, Philip and Edward Baldwin
(eds.), *Baldwin Papers: A Conservative
Statesman, 1908–1947*, Cambridge:
Cambridge University Press, 2004

JOURNALS

Daily Mail
Daily Mirror
Guardian
Life
Manchester Evening News
Morning Post
News of the World
Saga
Saturday Review
Spectator
Star-News
Strand
Telegraph
The New York Times
The Times

A NOTE ON SOURCES AND SUGGESTED FURTHER READING

The following is a general guide for readers wishing to find out more about Churchill's life during the different chapters' timeframes. The bibliography covers more broadly the range of works consulted for this book, including the majority of sources for quotes and extracts by others.

A key source for anyone writing about Churchill is of course the eight-volume official biography, *Winston S. Churchill* by Randolph S. Churchill and Martin Gilbert, which reproduces significant extracts from Churchill's correspondence and other communications in chronological progression. This structure is amplified in the extensive series of companion volumes, *The Churchill Documents*, each of which is keyed into a volume of the biography. *Churchill: A Photographic Portrait*, also by Martin Gilbert, acts as a superb sequence of captioned images that can be read in parallel with the biography, Gilbert's own stand-alone volume *Churchill: A Life*, and his personal selection of Churchill's writings, *Churchill: The Power of Words*. Churchill's daughter, Mary Soames, edited the definitive anthology of her parents' correspondence, entitled *Speaking for Themselves: The Personal Letters of Winston and Clementine Churchill*, as well as writing several other works about her family. In their selections of material, all these books also provide an overview of the breadth of material held at the Churchill Archives Centre, Cambridge.

In addition, the following works from which this book is drawn are suggested as further reading.

Chapter One
Childhood: 1874–1892

Winston Churchill's own account of his childhood, education and early military career can be found in his classic work, *My Early Life*, published in 1930. Family correspondence about his birth and the first years of his life features in *Winston S. Churchill: Youth 1874–1900*, the first volume of the Official Biography, and its related *Documents* volume.

Chapter Two
A Young Soldier: 1893–1900

Churchill's granddaughter Celia Sandys' book *From Winston with Love and Kisses* highlights some of the most charming examples of his writing and correspondence from the early years. This chapter also draws on Churchill's article 'American Intervention in Cuba', published in *Saturday Review* on 7 March 1896, his biography of his father, *Lord Randolph Churchill*, and his account of the conflict in the Sudan, *The River War*.

Chapter Three
Early Political Career: 1904–1914

The key volume for finding out more about Winston Churchill's first forays into politics is Randolph S. Churchill's *Winston S. Churchill: Young Statesman 1901–1914*, which benefits from being read alongside Mary Soames' *Speaking for Themselves*.

Chapter Four
The First World War: 1914–1918
Chapter Five
Rising Through the Ranks: 1919–1928

The titles above, and the relevant volumes of the Official Biography, are all rich in information on Winston's activities during and after the First World War. *The World Crisis* is his own account of the conflict and its aftermath. *Churchill's Great Contemporaries* (1937) draws together a number of writings on other prominent figures in this era. 'Each afternoon… "He's a bricklayer,"' was said by his grandson, Winston Churchill, when interviewed by Mary Riddell in the *Daily Telegraph*, 28 November 2008.

Chapter Six
The Wilderness Years: 1929–1939

Many of the same sources as Chapter Five are relevant for this period of Winston's life. Readers may also wish to consult Martin Gilbert, *Churchill and America*; and Churchill's collection of essays from the time, published as *Thoughts and Adventures* (1932), and William Manchester's *The Last Lion*.

Chapter Seven
The Second World War: 1939–1945

There are obviously countless sources for these years. The key volumes are of course Winston Churchill, *The Second World War, Volumes I–VI*, together with the works cited above. 'I was received pretty frostily… they accepted one' by Mary Soames appeared in *Saga*, October 2014.

Chapter Eight
The Post-War Years: 1946–1965

Authoritative accounts for the final chapter of Winston's life are *Speaking for Themselves* and *Winston S. Churchill: 'Never Despair' 1945–1965*, as well as Mary Soames's *Clementine Churchill: The Biography of a Marriage*. Celia Sandys' *Chasing Churchill* tells the stories of some of her grandfather's later travels. 'The span of mortals is short… better world or to oblivion' is taken from Winston Churchill, *Marlborough: His Life and Times*.

Also by Max Arthur:

The Busby Babes: Men of Magic
Above All, Courage: First Hand Accounts from the Falklands Front Line
Northern Ireland: Soldiers Talking
Men of the Red Beret
Lost Voices of the Royal Air Force
Lost Voices of the Royal Navy
When This Bloody War is Over: Soldier's Songs of the First World War
Symbol of Courage: A History of the Victoria Cross
Forgotten Voices of the Great War
Forgotten Voices of the Second World War
Last Post: The Final Word From Our First World War Soldiers
Lost Voices of the Edwardians
Faces of World War One
Dambusters: A Landmark Oral History
The Road Home: The Aftermath of the Great War Told by the Men and Women Who Survived It
Fighters Against Fascism: British Heroes of the Spanish Civil War
The Last of the Few: The Battle of Britain in the Words of the Pilots Who Won It
The Silent Day: A Landmark Oral History of D-Day on the Home Front

Index

Learn more about Winston Churchill

To explore a timeline of Winston Churchill's life and times, visit *www.churchillcentral.com*

Churchill Heritage Ltd works in association with his family to promote and support the good causes associated with his life and legacy. These include:

The Churchill Centre, the umbrella organisation for the Churchill enthusiast, dedicated to educating new generations in leadership and statesmanship. With branches throughout the United States and organisations in Australia, Canada, Israel, Portugal and the UK, the Centre combines being a membership organisation with charitable programmes and conferences, numerous regional events, tours, publication of the journal *Finest Hour*, awards and a public speaking competition. In the US it supports the National Churchill Library and Center at George Washington University, and in the UK it is a registered educational charity. *www.winstonchurchill.org*

The Winston Churchill Memorial Trust, set up as his living legacy, funds up to 150 British citizens each year from all walks of life to travel overseas on a project of their own choosing, in order to develop their knowledge and expertise, and bring back best practice for the benefit of others in their UK professions and communities. *www.wcmt.org.uk*

Churchill College, Cambridge, his national and Commonwealth memorial, was founded with the aim to benefit society through the advancement of education, learning and research, especially in the fields of science and technology. *www.chu.cam.ac.uk*

The Churchill Archives Centre, housed at Churchill College, contains nearly a million documents ranging from Churchill's first childhood letters, via his great war-time speeches, to the writings which earned him the Nobel Prize for Literature. Together with the papers of almost 600 important figures, they form an incomparable documentary treasure trove, a number of highlights from which are featured in this book. Sir Winston's personal papers are now available to academic institutions in digital form and with supporting materials at Churchill Archive On-line. *www.churchillarchive.com*

For a special selection of archive materials developed and resourced for schools, visit *www.churchillarchiveforschools.com*

Places to visit include:

Churchill War Rooms, part of Imperial War Museums in London, includes the original Cabinet War Rooms, the wartime bunker which sheltered Churchill and his staff during the Blitz. These historic rooms once buzzed with planning and plotting, strategies and secrets. Today visitors can explore the underground headquarters for themselves, see where Churchill and his War Cabinet met, sometimes late into the night, and look through the lens of history into the Map Room, where the books and charts have remained exactly where they were left on the day the lights were switched off in 1945. The Churchill Museum, also part of Churchill War Rooms, has a vast collection of objects, which together explore the stories of Churchill's life and legacy. *www.iwm.org.uk*

Chartwell, Churchill's house in Kent, which is now preserved as a historic property by the National Trust. Offering unique insights into his character and family life, this was the place into which he put so much of his time, energy and love; from the walls, to lakes and the house, to his books and the largest collection of his paintings in the world, together with a wonderful array of Churchillian artefacts, gifts from around the world and family treasures. *www.nationaltrust.org.uk/chartwell/*

Blenheim Palace, his Oxfordshire birthplace, is a World Heritage Site and home to the 12th Duke and Duchess of Marlborough. Grandson of the 7th duke, Churchill spent a considerable amount of time at the Palace throughout his life and proposed to his wife Clementine in the Temple of Diana. *www.blenheimpalace.com*

America's **National Churchill Museum** is located on the campus of Westminster College in Fulton, Missouri, where Churchill gave his famous 'Iron Curtain' speech, The Sinews of Peace, in 1946, a defining moment in the Cold War. Housed in the former City of London church of St Mary the Virgin Aldermanbury, designed by Sir Christopher Wren, moved stone by stone to Westminster's campus and rebuilt to Wren's original specifications, the museum brings to life the story of Winston Churchill and the world he knew through the imaginative and innovative use of technology. *www.nationalchurchillmuseum.org*

Sir Winston Churchill's published works are available in print and in ebook form from the world's leading publishers. His eight-volume Official Biography and its Companion Volumes are published by Hillsdale College. *www.hillsdale.edu/outreach/churchill-project/home* *www.rosettabooks.com*

Think Like Churchill is an app which allows you to take part in the challenges that Winston faced throughout his life. You will learn more about Churchill's life as you explore his leadership style and decision-making process. See how closely your judgements match his with in-depth analysis from an expert psychologist. Inspired by Boris Johnson's *The Churchill Factor*, it brings biographical and historical context to each scenario with the ultimate goal of improving your own decision-making skills. *www.thinklikechurchill.com*

Acknowledgements

Selected excerpts from speeches, speech notes, dispatches, journalism, letters and works of Sir Winston Churchill reproduced with permission of Curtis Brown, London, on behalf of The Estate of Winston S. Churchill. © The Estate of Winston S. Churchill

Selected excerpts from *Winston S. Churchill: The Official Biography* by Randolph S. Churchill and Martin Gilbert reproduced with permission of Curtis Brown, London, on behalf of C&T Publications Limited © C&T Publications Limited

BRDW: Broadwater Collection
Images originating from the Broadwater Collection (BRDW), held at the Churchill Archives Centre, Cambridge, are reproduced with permission of Curtis Brown, London on behalf of the Broadwater Collection.

CHAR: Chartwell Trust Papers, 1874–1945
Images originating from the Chartwell Trust Papers (CHAR), held at the Churchill Archives Centre, Cambridge, are reproduced with permission of Curtis Brown, London on behalf of the Sir Winston Churchill Archive Trust. The words of Sir Winston Churchill © The Estate of Winston S. Churchill. The words of Lord Randolph Churchill © The Master, Fellows, and Scholars of Churchill College, Cambridge.

CHUR: Churchill Papers, 1945–1965
Images originating from the Churchill Papers (CHAR), held at the Churchill Archives Centre, Cambridge, are reproduced with permission of Curtis Brown, London on behalf of the Sir Winston Churchill Archive Trust. The words of Sir Winston Churchill © The Estate of Winston S. Churchill.

CSCT: The Papers of Clementine Ogilvy Spencer-Churchill, Baroness Spencer-Churchill of Chartwell
Images originating from The Papers of Clementine Ogilvy Spencer-Churchill, Baroness Spencer-Churchill of Chartwell held at the Churchill Archives Centre, Cambridge, are reproduced with permission of Curtis Brown, London on behalf of The Master, Fellows, and Scholars of Churchill College, Cambridge. The words of Baroness Spencer-Churchill © The Master, Fellows, and Scholars of Churchill College, Cambridge.

CHPH: Churchill Press Photographs, 1876–1965
Images originating from the Churchill Press Photographs collection, held at the Churchill Archives Centre, Cambridge, are reproduced with permission of Curtis Brown, London on behalf of The Master, Fellows, and Scholars of Churchill College, Cambridge.

WHCL: Winston Churchill Additional Collection
Images originating from the Winston Churchill Additional Collection, held at the Churchill Archives Centre, Cambridge, are reproduced with permission of Curtis Brown, London on behalf of The Master, Fellows, and Scholars of Churchill College, Cambridge. The photograph of Sir Winston Churchill's cigar is reproduced with thanks to Mr Paul Keane.

All rights in all third party copyright holders works as quoted in this book are reserved to the respective copyright holders.

PICTURE CREDITS

age fotostock Keystone Archives 2, 187. **Alamy** Keystone Pictures USA 249; nsf 239; Pictorial Press Ltd. 68; War Archive 43. **BNPS** 31; BlenheimPalace 260. **Bridgeman Images** Chartwell, Kent, UK/ The Churchill Collection/National Trust Photographic Library/Derrick E. Witty 92, 102; Private Collection 13 above, 14; Private Collection/Photo © Christie's Images 37, 66; Private Collection/The Stapleton Collection 10; The Illustrated London News Picture Library, London, UK 224. **Broadwater Collection** 7 above left, 7 below right, 8, 16, 22 below, 24 above, 28 left, 28 right, 42, 43 above, 46, 47, 53, 56 above, 63, 82, 112, 114, 115, 117, 120 below, 122, 123, 124 below, 127, 130, 135, 136, 137 above, 145, 157 above, 157 below, 173 above, 184 above, 189 above, 194, 198, 202, 205, 215, 223. **Chartwell Trust Papers, 1874–1945** 12, 18, 19, 23, 25, 30, 36, 48 left, 48 right, 56 below, 70-71, 76 below, 77, 95, 148, 153 (courtesy of the New York Historical Society), 171, 175, 178, 190, 199, 200, 201. **Churchill Papers, 1945–1965** 69, 174, 222, 227, 233, 254 above. **Churchill Press Photographs, 1876–1965** 76 above, 78, 212. **Condé Nast Publications** Edward Steichen/Vanity Fair. © Condé Nast. 154. **Corbis** 21, 210 above, 228; Bettmann 7 below left, 140, 146 above right, 168, 207, 221 above; Hulton-Deutsch Collection 214, 243; J. E. Purdy/Bettmann 7 centre left, 57; Lebrecht Music & Arts/Lebrecht Music & Arts 44-45. **Getty Images** A. Hudson/ Topical Press Agency/Hulton Archive 155; A. R. Coster/Topical Press Agency 7 centre right, 106; A. R. Tanner/Fox Photos/Hulton Archive 161; Buyenlarge 62; Capt. Horton/IWM via Getty Images 173 below; Central Press 73, 87, 246 above, 246 below; Central Press/Archive Photos 230; CPT TANNER - No 2 Army Film/ AFP 166, 206; Davis/Topical Press Agency 138-139; Derek Berwin/Fox Photos/Hulton Archive 247; Douglas Miller/Keystone/ Hulton Archive 248 below; Fox Photos 132-133, 202-203, 261; Galerie Bilderwelt 183; H. F. Davis/Topical Press Agency/ Hulton Archive 163; Hulton Archive 11, 17, 54-55, 60, 85, 89, 90-91, 104, 105, 126, 177; Imagno 142; Keystone 110, 151, 152 below; Keystone-France/Gamma-Keystone via Getty Images 108, 113 below, 128-129, 131, 208-209, 211, 229, 238; Kurt Hutton/ Picture Post 226; Lt. C J Ware/IWM via Getty Images 185; Major Horton/IWM via Getty Images 213 above; Mark Kauffman/ Time & Life Pictures 231, 232; Mondadori Collection 162 above; Mondadori Portfolio via Getty Images 220; New York Times Co. 137 below; OFF/AFP 241; Photo12/UIG 196 left; Planet News Archive/SSPL 156 above; Popperfoto 160, 164, 172, 176, 193, 234-235; RDA 251 above; Terry Fincher/Express/ Hulton Archive 253; Terry O'Neill/Hulton Archive 252; Thomas D. Mcavoy/The LIFE Picture Collection 186; Time Life Pictures/Pictures Inc./The LIFE Picture Collection 144, 165; Time Life Pictures/ The LIFE Images Collection 156 below; Topical Press Agency 88, 96; Topical Press Agency/Hulton Archive 162 below; ullstein bild/ullstein bild via Getty Images 74-75; Universal History Archive 49; Universal

Author's Acknowledgements

History Archive/UIG via Getty images 15 left. **Heritage Assets Limited** 26-27, 27 above right. **Library of Congress** 116, 180-181, 245. **Mary Evans Picture Library** 67; Grenville Collins Postcard Collection 24 below; Illustrated London News Ltd 15 right; Illustrated London News Ltd. 20-21, 80, 94, 103, 158-159; John Frost Newspapers 52; Photo Union Collection 225 above. **Mirrorpix** 7 above right, 32, 39, 83, 84, 99, 111, 118, 125, 147, 149, 218, 244; Barham 250; Birmingham Post and Mail 204-205; Collect 35 left; Daily Mirror 124 above; Edwards 242; Official 179, 189 below, 191 above, 195 above, 195 below, 196, 197 right, 210 below, 216; Philip Zec 188; Tommy Atiken 107. **Peregrine Churchill Papers** 86. **Press Association Images** 254 below, AP 152 above, 182, 192, 213 below, 251 below; Barratts/S&G Barratts/ EMPICS Archive 7 centre, 58, 72; Len Putnam/AP 150; Leslie Priest/AP 236; PA/ PA Archive 54, 79, 97, 113 above, 121, 225, 240; Personalities/Topham Picturepoint 41. **Randolph Churchill Papers** 119. **Reproduced by kind permission of the Keepers and Governors of Harrow School** 22 above, 29 above, 29 below. **Reproduced with the kind permission of his Grace the Duke of Marlborough, Blenheim Palace Image Library** 13 below. **Rex Features** 120 above; British Pathé 184 below; Courtesy Everett Collection 191 below; Edwin Sampson/Daily Mail 255; Staff/ Daily Mail 256. **Sandhurst Collection, Royal Military Academy Sandhurst** 34. **Science and Society Picture Library** National Media Museum 257. **The Papers of Clementine Ogilvy Spencer-Churchill, Baroness Spencer-Churchill of Chartwell** 61, 64-65, 98. **TopFoto** 169, 237, 248 above, 258-259; Imagno/Austrian Archives 143; The Granger Collection 38; Topham Picturepoint 40, 81, 100-101. **Winston Churchill Additional Collection** 146 above left, 146 below, 170, 221 below.

I would like to thank my editor, Trevor Davies, at Octopus Publishing who kept a steady and positive approach throughout, and particularly while waiting patiently for the final chapters. My thanks also to Alex Stetter, who diligently amended chapters, and Caroline Taggart, who has enhanced the book with her astute copy editing. Jennifer Veall also worked tirelessly researching and wading through mountains of Churchill images.

The book was conceived by my agent, Gordon Wise of Curtis Brown, after a conversation with Trevor Davies at the Serpentine Gallery on the occasion of the Octopus summer party, six months before the commencement of marking the many Churchillian anniversaries that were to fall in 2015: the 75 years since Churchill's coming into the premiership in 1940, the seventieth anniversary of the end of the Second World War in 1945, and the half century since his death in 1965 and its era-defining State Funeral. Gordon, who also represents the Churchill Estate, has been a great support throughout the writing of this book. I'm extremely grateful to the staff of the Churchill Archives Centre in Cambridge, particularly Natalie Adams, Katharine Thomson and Sarah Lewery, for their support in sourcing original documents and family photographs, as well as facilitating the capture of artefacts from their collection which are seen for the first time in this book. John David Olsen and Paul Courtenay of the Churchill Centre have kindly assisted in reading the text, and Churchill Heritage has, with the support of Richard Pike, arranged for the clearance of the Churchill family materials featured in this book.

Rose Riley and Nick Baldock helped with both the typing and the early research. I particularly want to thank Sorcha Berry-Varley. who worked closely with me and produced invaluable research material.

I would also like to thank my friends Ruth Cowen, Lucia Corti, Deborah Moggach and Susan Jeffreys for their love and support.

My brother Adrian was also at hand with information on the military aspects of WSC's life, and I thank him. Since my first book in 1985, Don and Liz McClen have always been there and their friendship has been invaluable.

My final thanks go to Lady Esther Gilbert, who has kept the spirit of her husband and my dear friend, Martin, very much alive.